LAWYERS,
MONEY,
AND SUCCESS

LAWYERS, MONEY, AND SUCCESS

The Consequences of Dollar Obsession

Macklin Fleming

Quorum Books
Westport, Connecticut • London

Library of Congress Cataloging-in-Publication Data

Fleming, Macklin, 1911–
    Lawyers, money, and success : the consequences of dollar obsession
    / Macklin Fleming.
      p. cm.
    Includes bibliographical references and index.
    ISBN 1–56720–134–2 (alk. paper)
    1. Practice of law—Economic aspects—United States. 2. Lawyers—
    Fees—United States. 3. Legal ethics—United States. I. Title.
    KF315.F58   1997
    174'.3'0973—dc21   96–54286

British Library Cataloguing in Publication Data is available.

Library of Congress Catalog Card Number: 96–54286
ISBN: 1–56720–134–2

First published in 1997

Quorum Books, 88 Post Road West, Westport, CT 06881
An imprint of Greenwood Publishing Group, Inc.

Printed in the United States of America

The paper used in this book complies with the
Permanent Paper Standard issued by the National
Information Standards Organization (Z39.48–1984).

10 9 8 7 6 5 4 3 2 1

Contents

Preface

On returning to the trial court after many years' service as an appellate judge, my curiosity was aroused by the phenomenon of premium legal fees routinely charged by major law firms for work that was often mediocre, and occasionally less than mediocre.

Paralleling this phenomenon was an increased public distrust of lawyers, a distrust that had reached the point where bar associations and lawyers' lobbyists felt it necessary to undertake expensive public-relations campaigns to improve the image of lawyers, campaigns received by the general public with indifference or with quiet snickers and the occasional horse laugh. At the same time more and more lawyers were expressing their discontent with the legal profession. Rarely were these developments linked together.

In seeking an explanation for the continued existence of premium legal fees for observably mediocre legal work, I found that, like pulling on the loose end of a tangled ball of yarn, the subject of excessive legal fees led to lawyer dominance over fee setting, thence to lawyer-client relationships, to law firm organization, to the economics of legal services, and from there to the effect of legal economics on lawyer discontent. Each of these subjects merits years of observation and study, during which initial conclusions might need constant revision to accommodate the fluidity of the subject and the rapidity of its evolution. This task I have not attempted. Rather, I have sought to outline the underlying causes of inflated legal fees and indicate how the profession is likely to evolve. Examples given are illustrative rather than exhaustive.

Several authors have recently explored the role of lawyers today, among them President-emeritus Derek Bok of Harvard, Ambassador Sol M. Linowitz, Dean Anthony T. Kronman, Professor Mary Ann Glendon, and Judge Richard A. Posner.[1] What need for another book? Two reasons. Unwelcome news requires more than one Cassandra to be believed. And since accurate information about legal fees and law firm profits is difficult to obtain, evaluations from different vantage points are essential, much as the combined perceptions of six blind men are needed to provide a reasonably accurate picture of the elephant, in this case the elephant of present-day law practice. My vantage point is 55 years in the law, half in public and private law practice in New York, Washington, San Francisco, and Los Angeles offices, large, medium, and small; and half on the bench as a trial and appellate judge in the California courts.

For valuable comments on the text of this work my great thanks to my wife, Polly, and for cogent analysis of its arguments and conclusions my thanks to Roy H. Aaron, Ronald S. Beard, Arnold Beichman, Jerome C. Byrne, Lloyd N. Cutler, Donald P. deBrier, Martha M. Fleming, William D. Gould, David Y. Handelman, Sanford J. Hillsberg, A. Andrew Hauk, Derek W. Hunt, Oscar M. Ruebhausen, Joseph F. Troy, and David J. Wohlberg.

Responsibility for errors in the text or fallacies in its argument and conclusions is mine alone.

1

The Paradox

Complaints by clients about excessive legal fees have been in existence for at least 2,500 years, ever since Aesop's two disputants each received half an oyster shell while the lawyer kept the pearl as his fee. But with the rise in the last 30 years of the large law firm as the mainstream vessel for delivery of legal services, complaints about excessive legal fees have reached a new pitch. During that same period delivery of legal services became big business. Projected gross revenues for legal services in 1994 were $97 billion, a greater amount than the revenues of such major industries as air transport ($78 billion), pharmaceuticals ($70 billion), and textiles ($69 billion).[1] In 1994 the largest of the nation's law firms reportedly had annual gross revenues of $582 million while 100 firms had grosses in excess of $76 million.[2] In 1995 the largest law firm had over 1,750 lawyers, 250 firms had 131 lawyers or more,[3] and over 700 firms had 52 lawyers or more.[4] During the past 45 years legal fees have increased well beyond any increase in the rate of inflation, and their percentage of the national income has tripled. Yet this increase in fees occurred during a period in which the number of lawyers quadrupled, and their ratio in the general population almost tripled.[5] What has happened to the law of supply and demand?

To some extent discussion of excessive legal fees must be impressionistic, in that accurate information about fees and receipts of law firms and their subsequent division among lawyers within firms is as difficult to obtain as accurate economic and political information from Beijing. Privately-owned law firms do not issue public reports of receipts, profits, and individual earnings of their lawyers, or file financial documents from which this information can be gleaned. At best we have occasional glimpses of specific receipts, sometimes in proxy statements of publicly-held corporations reporting moneys paid to law firms, sometimes in extraneous litigation to which lawyers are parties (divorce, bankruptcy, internal law firm disputes), sometimes in fee applications to the courts, and, recently but less reliably, in the reports of law-trade publications, which in turn are based on law firms' own unaudited representations.

An added difficulty in evaluating legal fees is that fees can be classified as excessive only when related to work done, legal skills required, difficulties encountered, and results achieved. Here again, exact information is hard to obtain in that the product of lawyer activity is often intangible and its subject matter frequently confidential. Moreover, legal fees cannot be considered in a vacuum apart from methods used and organizations created to deliver legal services, any more than rates of interest can be considered apart from prevailing commercial practices in moneylending and the organizations and procedures that facilitate this activity. We must extend our inquiry to past methods of delivery of legal services and their evolution into the methods used today. A brief glimpse at recent history is instructive.

2

Invention of the Corporate Law Firm and Its Evolution into the Large Law Firm

The legal profession we know began in England with the medieval organization of lawyers into guilds, whose members were given a monopoly of the right to appear in the law courts, but who each practiced law on his own. Lawyers were answerable for their conduct to their guilds and to the judges. This scheme for delivery of legal services by individual lawyers made its way to this country and continued virtually unchanged to the end of the nineteenth century. During that period the most significant change in the status of American lawyers was their growing influence and importance in the community, which in turn led to relaxation of guild and judicial controls over their activities. The format of individual practice dominated, and the few legal partnerships that existed were usually transitory, of no particular prestige or identity apart from the individual lawyers who made up their membership. As late as 1900 in New York City what is now the Cravath Swaine law firm consisted of 13 lawyers—three seniors, three juniors, and seven assistants—and the firm of Sullivan & Cromwell totaled 14 lawyers.[1] Judging from the frequent changes in the names and composition of most such firms, law practice remained an individual enterprise in which for temporary convenience lawyers occasionally grouped together in partnerships. Juniors customarily assisted seniors during a brief apprenticeship before setting up on their own. As defined by Henry L. Stimson, a member of the New York firm still bearing his name, a law firm consisted of a group of gentlemen practicing law together. The stuff of law practice was mainly advocacy, and in the closing decades of the nineteenth century the giants of the bar, Elihu Root, Joseph H. Choate, and the young Charles Evans Hughes, were fully at home in the courtroom.

Yet about the turn of the century was born a revolution in the delivery of legal services, one of the great creations of the twentieth century, comparable to that of Rockefeller in the distribution of oil and Ford in the manufacture of motor vehicles. This invention was the corporate law firm, an instrument designed to deliver legal services for the organization, aggregation, consolidation, and reorganization of the large amounts of capital needed to operate national and international businesses under centralized control and conditions of limited liability. In addition, the corporate law firm undertook to counsel corporate clients on legal dealings with public authorities, competitors, debtors, and creditors.

Through expanded use of the mechanism of the private corporation, the corporate law firm was able to deliver and service a standardized superior product for the conduct of large-scale business enterprise and do this at a lower price than that charged for the legal mechanisms (partnerships and trusts) theretofore used to aggregate capital at retail. The corporate law firm made itself into a permanent organization for effective, continuing delivery of corporate-law services through the following steps: employment at a premium wage of the most promising young lawyers entering the legal ranks, specialization in corporate work, subdivision among its lawyers of component parts of a large transaction (a railroad reorganization, an industrial merger, a multimillion-dollar flotation of securities), elimination of nepotism, and avoidance of legal activity outside its own specialized field. Under the leadership of such men as Walter S. Carter, Paul Cravath, Louis D. Brandeis, and Andrew Squire, the corporate law firm largely superseded individual practicing lawyers in its field, and its members enjoyed considerably higher incomes than did lawyers engaged in other legal activities.[2]

The effectiveness and profitability of the corporate law firm may be illustrated by a hypothetical example based on constant-dollar charges for comparable legal services. To incorporate a new Delaware corporation, the corporate law firm through use of a specialized corporate lawyer might charge $250 for legal work taking about an hour. To do the same, but probably less skillfully, a general practitioner might take five hours and charge $500.[3] The client would get from the corporate law firm at least a comparable and probably a superior product at half the price charged by the general practitioner. Assuming both had profitable employment for five hours that day, the corporate law firm would take in $1,250 and the general practitioner only $500. In such fashion the corporate law firm was able to deliver within its sphere quicker and probably better legal service at lower cost to its client than could the general practitioner, while at the same time earning more money for its lawyers. It was of no consequence to the client that the corporate law firm charged a premium price that could make its lawyers rich, so long as the firm delivered a superior product at a lower client-cost.

Paralleling the rise of the corporate law firm was the appearance of the lawyer counselor, usually the head of a corporate law firm, who advised business leaders on major business decisions. The function of lawyer counselor arose at a time when business leaders, including the most successful, were often men of limited formal education and limited experience apart from their particular business activity. They came from the machine shop (Henry Ford), the retail counter (J. C. Penney), the bookkeeper's stool (John D. Rockefeller), the foundry (Charles W. Schwab of U.S. Steel). Such businessmen, generally inexperienced in the wider world of politics, group relationships, monetary policies, and international affairs, grew accustomed to seeking advice on such matters from their lawyers, these being the principal individuals of wider experience with whom business leaders came into regular contact. Out of need and from availability was born the lawyer counselor, who became an instant hit and enjoyed a run well into the 1960s. The relationship was akin to that of European kings and their clergy in the eleventh century. The latter were literate, the former often not. To the clergy as chancellors were entrusted the mechanics of structuring the kingdom and recommending solutions for all nonmilitary problems. In similar fashion the lawyer counselor became a modern-day chancellor, who had the ear of the monarch and undertook to guide him in all fields outside his specific business activity. In time reliance of the monarch-business leader on his chancellor-counselor became habitual. Thus it became inconceivable that David Sarnoff (RCA) would make a major move without consulting his lawyer John Cahill, that Harrison Williams (public utilities) would move without consulting John Foster Dulles, that Harry Cohn (Columbia Pictures) would move without consulting Mendel Silberberg. These lawyer counselors became powerful figures in their own right, ranking on a par with railroad moguls, steel barons, and the princes of international finance, frequently serving as chairmen of the boards of art museums, symphony orchestras, opera associations, and other nonprofit institutions interested in cultivating access to the rich and powerful. This special relationship between business leader and lawyer counselor strongly fortified the position and prestige of the latter's corporate law firm.

During the first half of the century the corporate law firm tended to stick to corporate work. Its other legal activities served primarily to accommodate its corporate clients. Office counseling, document drafting, and private negotiation dominated its activities, while courtroom activity played a distinctly secondary role. The number of corporate law firms in the country remained small, there being in 1940 fewer than a dozen firms of 50 or more lawyers, all east of the Mississippi, plus several dozen smaller corporate law firms located in commercial and industrial centers throughout the country. During this period the sole practitioner and the small law firm engaged in general practice remained the dominant elements in the delivery of legal services.

But with the second half of the century the corporate law firm began to extend the characteristic features of corporate law practice to other kinds of legal work. Its techniques—the performance of specialized services in a narrow field, subdivided into tasks, carried out with the assistance of young lawyers whose histories promised superior talents, and delivered at premium fees but with lower net costs to the client—were first used in such related areas as taxation, trusts, and banking, whose legal activities tended to involve repetitive use of complicated but similar patterns within a narrow framework of rights and duties. In these limited areas the corporate law firm could still plausibly assert that through specialization and subdivision of labor it could outpace the general practitioner and give the client a superior product at a lower net cost, even while charging premium prices for its services. But during the past 30 years it has extended the use of these techniques to all areas of legal practice, most notably into the trial work that constitutes a major share of law practice. Simultaneously, the corporate law firm began, like a giant vacuum cleaner, to sweep every type of profitable legal business into its bag by a continuous expansion of facilities, offices, and personnel, and as new areas of legal activity showed promise of high profitability, it moved to take them in as well. In such fashion the corporate law firm evolved into the large law firm of today, active in all legal areas where large profits appear probable.

3

Emergence of the Large Law Firm as the Dominant Element of the Profession

Some discussion of the general forces that have brought about concentration and centralization of legal-service providers will help clarify current operations of large law firms and suggest the course of their future development.

The basic cause of legal concentration and centralization is the explosion of knowledge that has occurred in the modern world and the resulting fragmentation of specific skills needed to deal effectively with each segment of that knowledge. Not since Dante's time has any one person been able to know all that is known to man. To make knowledge manageable it became essential to divide the mansion of knowledge into separate apartments of philosophy, theology, medicine, law, engineering, arts and architecture, natural sciences. Each apartment served reasonably well until the nineteenth century, when it became necessary to divide most of them into separate rooms and later still to subdivide the rooms into separate cubicles. The rate of subdivision varied greatly among disciplines, with natural sciences taking the lead and theology bringing up the rear. In this process law was more laggard than most, and at the end of the nineteenth century a lawyer could still claim to be reasonably conversant with all aspects of law and competent to prepare documents and give advice on most legal matters. The body of the law was of manageable size. For example, all laws of the United States (as distinguished from those of individual states) were published in one volume of moderate size. Government regulations, executive orders, court rules, government agency advisory opinions, for all practical purposes did not exist. The same lawyer could write a will, form a partnership, defend or prosecute a criminal case, handle a divorce, clear a title, and secure a municipal franchise. When an unfamiliar subject arose, a day's homework usually sufficed to equip him to handle the problem.

Those days will not return. As the complications of society multiplied, a huge mass of new law was created. Individual lawyers found themselves in a losing struggle to keep current in all areas of the law, and by 1990 the American Bar Association had recognized twenty-four categories of legal specialization, with more waiting in the wings.[1] To remain professionally competent, a lawyer has had no choice but to concentrate in a particular area of law and relinquish even a general familiarity with other areas. Legal specialization is not a matter of any particular strangeness or abstruseness of specialty but one of lawyer and client economics. Today's lawyer cannot afford to spend the three months, six months, or two years needed to acquire competency in some unfamiliar legal area merely to handle a single transaction. Neither does a client expect to pay fees to support his or her lawyer during this learning period. For example, it is theoretically possible for a corporate lawyer without bankruptcy experience to shepherd a corporation through bankruptcy, but the task would require months of intensive work by the corporate lawyer to educate himself in the substance and practice of bankruptcy law to deal competently with his client's problems. Economic considerations make legal specialization a necessity, both in private law offices and in large public and corporate legal offices such as those of the Los Angeles District Attorney, the U.S. Attorney General in Washington, and the law departments of Exxon and DuPont.

Arrival of legal specialization has had a major impact on both the seller of services (the lawyer) and their buyer (the client). In an earlier age a lawyer needed two basic assets to conduct a successful law practice—knowledge of the law and paying clients. Prior to the age of specialization a lawyer could acquire sufficient legal knowledge by serving a relatively brief apprenticeship in the office of an established lawyer before starting on his own. On opening his office he could, with the exercise of reasonable diligence, secure clients through friends, acquaintances, civic activities, and referrals of overflow business from senior lawyers. These arrangements no longer serve. The legal knowledge a beginning lawyer now acquires by working for others equips him to handle only a narrow segment of legal problems. The clientele that might need such specialized services has become equally narrow and is usually unreachable through friends and acquaintances. Operating under the old system, today's legal specialist could spend a substantial part of her time awaiting the arrival of clients who never came, in that the better mousetrap that did the job in Emerson's time catches few clients for the legal specialist. Matters have also changed for clients. In an earlier age a client could consult his own trusted lawyer for all problems, confident they would be competently handled by that lawyer. Today, if he consults the lawyer he knows, he cannot be certain his lawyer possesses any familiarity with his problem or even knows enough about it to refer him to a lawyer who does. It is likely the client will end up with a complete stranger, of whose competence, reputation, and integrity he knows little.

Enter the large law firm, equipped to solve both the problem of the lawyer getting business and that of the client seeking competent and reliable representation for his specific problem. In essence, today's large law firm is an aggregation of specialists who have combined under one banner to produce a full-service firm covering all major substantive and procedural specialties, including corporation law, bankruptcy, real estate, intellectual property, litigation, taxation, trusts, and so on. It may contain lawyers who specialize in the legal problems of a specific industry, such as electronics, banking, entertainment, health care, and the like. With the immediate availability of this personnel a client's problem can be expeditiously diagnosed, appropriate specialists consulted as needed, and immediate steps taken to address his problem. The firm is large enough to handle the complex problems arising from today's concentration and centralization of economic activities. And it can minimize the cost of coordinating legal projects involving the services of multiple lawyers more effectively than can individual lawyers in temporary collaboration.

For lawyers, the large law firm solves multiple problems. By means of the law firm the lawyer with more time than clients and the lawyer with more clients than time can combine activities to their mutual benefit. Where receipt of fees is long-delayed—in bankruptcies, class actions, reorganizations, contingent fees—the large law firm has access to credit in amounts an individual lawyer does not. Finally, the firm smooths the inevitable ups and downs of a particular specialty by creating a profit-sharing system among its lawyers designed to average feast and famine. For clients, the large law firm provides one-stop shopping—immediate access to competent providers of the specific types of legal services they need, from whom they can obtain timely and accurate diagnoses of their problems without the need for lawyer education at client expense. To return to our bankruptcy example, reference to a bankruptcy specialist within the law firm would result in immediate instead of delayed action, in knowledgeable representation, and in a consequent saving in total cost.

In sum, the large law firm at its best functions as a giant produce market under one roof and one management through which customers of all sorts (clients) and purveyors of all sorts (lawyers) can transact business. The market's management provides assurance to buyers of quality and honest dealing, of receipt of honest weight at posted prices. The market's reputation attracts customers for its various purveyors. The grocer who deals in packaged goods can refer customers with other specific wants to the nearby counters of the butcher, baker, and candlestick maker, according to the customer's desires and needs. The growth in specialties necessarily produces growth in size. The American large law firm has proved a formidable success, and the fact that it is being copied by lawyers from Brussels to London to Toronto to Sydney is not only proof of its worth but a strong indicator it is here to stay.

The trend toward concentration of professionals in large groups is not unique to the legal profession. Group organization and professional referral within the group can be found among organizations of accountants, doctors, architects, engineers, and so on. In these professions demands for services tend to gravitate to a central market, where they are sorted out and routed to the particular specialists equipped to render the desired services, such as the architect who specializes in racetracks or the one who designs prisons. In this consolidation of smaller into larger entities, these professionals in turn are merely following earlier paths blazed by manufacturing, distribution, and financial enterprises.

Thus far we have not quantified the large law firm. Such a firm usually possesses two identifying characteristics: It covers all basic areas of legal practice (the full-service law firm), and it has become too large for any one person to monitor all its activities. Because the support staff of a large law firm normally exceeds the number of its lawyers, a 50-lawyer firm will comprise about 125 persons for whose activities the firm is responsible. A total of 125 persons engaged in providing a diversity of services represents the approximate maximum number that may be effectively controlled by one person. Thus, 50 lawyers and above provides a suitable identification for the large law firm, and it is the figure used here. On this basis the number of large law firms during the past half-century has expanded exponentially, the dozen firms of 50 or more lawyers in 1940 having grown to over 800,[2] if we count separately the offices of multicity firms. This explosive growth in the size of large law firms can be shown by comparing lawyer numbers in specific law firms in 1937 with their numbers in 1995:

City	Firm	1937	1995
New York	Sullivan & Cromwell	28 partners	109 partners
	Davis Polk	20 partners	109 partners
	Skadden Arps	—	252 partners

San Francisco	Pillsbury Madison	8 partners	243 partners
	Brobeck Phleger	6 partners	150 partners
Los Angeles	O'Melveny & Myers	33 lawyers	552 lawyers
	Gibson Dunn	28 lawyers	672 lawyers
Cleveland	Squire Sanders	42 lawyers	358 lawyers
	Jones Day (formerly Tolles Hogsett)	26 lawyers	1118 lawyers[3]

The emergence of 800 large law offices has revolutionized the prevailing structure of the legal profession and made these offices the dominant vehicles for delivery of legal services. Today's legal profession of well over 800,000 lawyers may be roughly divided into five principal groups:

- Lawyers in large, privately-owned law firms (15 percent)
- Lawyers in individual practice and small firms (45 percent)
- Lawyers employed by private corporations (13 percent)
- Lawyers employed by public agencies (12 percent)
- Judicial, miscellaneous, and inactive (15 percent)[4]

The once dominant group of individual lawyers and small firms, formerly 75 percent to 80 percent of all lawyers, has steadily lost and continues to lose ground to the four other groups, so that it now constitutes a minority. Although large law firms employ only 15 percent of all lawyers, their sphere of influence is augmented by those of their lawyers who move to and from public employment, to and from corporate employment, to and from small law firms. Perhaps 20 percent of all lawyers are now or at some time have been affiliated with large law firms. These firms have become so dominant that they monopolize the mainstream of private practice, relegating individual practicing lawyers and small law firms to secondary channels of diminishing importance in the legal world.

This major change in the structure of the legal profession parallels similar changes in the social order, which have brought about increased collectivization and centralization and an increased enforcement of legal rights and duties through collective and centralized means. Rights arising in the principal areas of economic life and well-being—employment, working conditions, business activity, savings, investment, pensions, government obligations and benefits—which were formerly enforced by individual action, are now normally pursued collectively through group, class, union, trade association, or representative effort. Collective action substantially raises the stakes in any given controversy, with the result that all sides seek out the best available legal specialists, who are usually to be found in large law firms. For example, disputes concerning individual rights in a pension fund may be so complex and so costly to pursue that individual vindication is impracticable and only collective action is feasible.

Of equal importance is the centralization in metropolises of control over economic activities. In today's small or medium-size Midwestern town the department store may be operated from Dallas, the manufacturing plant from Chicago, the largest labor union from New York, the bank from San Francisco, and grain-milling activities from Minneapolis. Major legal problems and disputes arising out of local operations will be forwarded to headquarters, thence to the organization's legal department or a large law firm in the headquarters area. With similar nationwide concentration in most major areas of economic life, profitable legal business gravitates to the large firms in metropolitan areas, while sole practitioners and small law firms, in small towns and metropolitan areas alike, are left with legal business arising from individual activities, such as local real estate transfers, local service businesses, domestic relations, personal injury claims, and individual criminal defense.

In such fashion has arisen what Heinz and Laumann identify as the two hemispheres of legal practice.[5] In the more prosperous northern hemisphere of collective and organizational practice are the large law firms and major corporate legal departments, increasing in size, prospering from the growing share of legal receipts originating from collective activities, and benefiting from the concentration of legal business in metropolitan areas. In the southern hemisphere are the solo lawyers and small law firms, competing for the decreasing share of legal business that derives from individuals. The advertising of attorneys in the Yellow Pages of any California telephone book provides a snapshot of the private sector of this southern hemisphere. Also located in the southern hemisphere are most lawyers employed by public entities or paid from public funds, a group that includes prosecutors, public defenders, and public agency lawyers. Each year the income of lawyers in the southern hemisphere declines in relation to that of lawyers in large law firms and corporate legal departments.[6]

There are, of course, the conspicuous exceptions of a few lawyers in personal-injury and criminal-defense areas who reputedly make great sums of money, but these well-publicized exceptions divert our attention from the declining fortunes of most personal-injury and criminal-defense lawyers. In those areas, as in others, the large law firm continues its invasion of those specific types of legal activity that are proving profitable—recently, white-collar crime and contingent-fee actions in fraud and environmental-disaster claims. As noted by Sol Linowitz, the contingent fee moved upstairs when Cravath Swaine (New York) entered the savings-and-loan fraud litigation and Kirkland & Ellis (Chicago) began taking cases on speculation.[7]

Explosive growth in the size of large law firms has been accompanied by explosive growth in the size of their fees,[8] but in evaluating the extent of this increase we enter a largely unmapped domain, shrouded in mist and populated with uncommunicative inhabitants. Before comparing its contours with those known to us from the past, we must take into account the devaluation of money that reduced the purchasing power of the 1935 dollar to between nine and ten cents in 1995, resulting in more than a tenfold increase in the price level.[9] The loaf of bread or dozen eggs that cost ten or fifteen cents in 1935 may now cost $1.50 or more. Although not all prices move uniformly, some being affected by factors other than inflation, a great many, including those for personal services, remain closely tied to the general level of inflation or deflation. In the legal world this relationship to the general cost of living may be seen by comparing yearly salaries of judges in 1935 with those in 1995, which for federal district judges have risen from $10,000 to $130,600 and for Los Angeles Superior Court judges from $10,000 to $107,400, increases of thirteenfold and elevenfold, respectively, which approximate the tenfold-plus increase in the cost of living. The comparison between 1935 and 1995 of salaries paid to judges is easily made, because judges are performing the same duties in the same setting in both periods, and the amount of their salaries is public information.

But with respect to lawyers, changes in organization of the profession have been so rapid and the growth of legal business has been so extensive that exact comparisons of earnings in different periods are difficult to make—even assuming we possessed accurate information on earnings, which we do not. Nevertheless, we have one figure on which accurate information over an extended period of time is available, that of starting salaries for beginning lawyers in large New York City law firms. These are known and publicized by law students, by law school placement offices, and by the law firms themselves in their recruiting efforts. Factors contributing to secrecy about lawyers' earnings—individual prestige, law firm prestige, client comparisons, colleague comparisons—have not yet come into play. Yearly starting salaries for beginning lawyers in large New York law firms increased from $2,100 in 1935 to $4,200 in 1954, a 100 percent increase that closely paralleled the 96 percent increase in the Consumer Price Index for the same period.[10] But beginning in the early 1960s, these same salaries accelerated their increase to $85,000 in 1995,[11] a fortyfold increase over salaries of 1935 during a period when the Consumer Price Index increased only tenfold, that is, an increase four times the rate of inflation. Outside New York starting salaries for beginners at large law firms have been and continue to be somewhat lower, but their proportionate increase over earlier years is probably even greater than in New York. Since large law firms make a profit from marketing to clients the services of first- and second-year law graduates at charges as high as $150 and $180 an hour, we may infer that fees charged by large law firms for legal services have risen well above any increase in the rate of inflation, perhaps approaching the four times suggested by the salary increases for beginning lawyers. And both growth in the percentage of national income spent for legal services and growth in the total amounts spent for legal services confirm the conclusion that legal fees have sizably outpaced the general rate of inflation.[12] It is likewise clear that the average income in large law firms is considerably greater than that in small law firms and among sole practitioners.[13]

Thus far we have assumed that large law firms operate in their most cost-effective manner and have not inquired into possible weaknesses that might detract from their effectiveness. The first potential weakness, one we identify as cubicle vision, comes from a specialization so narrow that the lawyer in one cubicle does not understand what her neighbor in the adjoining cubicle is doing and may not even know what lawyers in other rooms and apartments of the law mansion are up to. As a consequence the specialist in one field may not recognize problems outside her specialty. For example, a business reorganization may be well conceived from the corporate point of view but ruinous from tax consequences of which the corporate lawyer is unaware. Similarly, a family business trust may be ideal to minimize taxes but disastrous in the event of future family dissention.

Specialization by itself does not provide a sufficient foundation for effective delivery of competent legal services. Legal specialists, like specialists in other fields of human activity—surgeons, psychiatrists, city planners, sociologists, termite inspectors—often suffer from cubicle vision and see the exercise of their specialty as the appropriate solution for most difficulties that come their way. Thus, the likely advice of the trial lawyer is "Sue the bastards"; of the office lawyer, "Negotiate"; of the corporate lawyer, "Reorganize"; of the tax lawyer, "Make a tax-deductible settlement"; of the probate lawyer, "Use a third-party trust." The broader view of a generalist is needed to sort out and evaluate the oft-conflicting advice of the specialists.

The generalist is a lawyer of comprehensive experience and demonstrated legal skills, who combines high standards with the ability to harmonize a diverse group of talented but sometimes temperamental specialists. In recent years the term *generalist* has acquired negative connotations, implying the limited skills of a nineteenth-century country doctor or a utility infielder capable of filling in but not holding down a permanent position. As used here, *generalist* means a person who has transcended the limitations of a particular specialty and acquired the capability of handling affairs of broader scope, much as a general officer in the Army has risen through mastery of one specialty (infantry, artillery, cavalry, supply) to command of their combined operations. The elusive qualities that constitute a generalist have often been described as mental ability allied with common sense. Yet common sense is frequently 180 degrees off-target. A better description is that of William James, who refers to these qualities as *intelligent intelligence*, which he identifies as intelligence that supplies the means and the standard of measurement to achieve a final purpose.[14] It is part natural talent and part acquired skill, which, like the playing of music, requires training and practice to perfect. Its raw materials may include varying proportions of logic, emotion, wit, inventiveness, conscience, perseverance, discipline, curiosity. James has another illuminating phrase pertinent to the idea of a generalist, *the knowing of things together*, the title of one of his essays.[15] But regardless of definition the quality of the fully-developed generalist is easy to recognize when we come in contact with it, in legal circles and elsewhere, and its value is demonstrated to us almost daily in affairs great and small. For example, aggressiveness in a lawyer is an admirable talent when exercised in the right place at the right time, but that same aggressiveness may be injurious and destructive when directed at clients, colleagues, or judges. To be effective, its productive use may require the participation of a generalist, much as General Patton needed the control of a Marshall and an Eisenhower to function at what he did best.[16] A large law firm needs both generalists and specialists to achieve and maintain integrity and quality control, to provide long-term perspective to clients, to curb rivalries of specialists pulling in different directions, and to exercise the necessary authority to put the overall interests of the firm and its clients ahead of those of any particular department or individual lawyer. To operate successfully over time a large law firm must have able generalists in charge.

In addition to cubicle vision, the second potential weakness of the large law firm is loss of cost-effectiveness to the client in its delivery of legal services. We have noted the sharp increases in large law firm fees during the past 30 years. It remains possible that current deliveries of legal services are so effective that clients continue to receive full value for the premium fees they have been paying, as had been the case earlier. To evaluate this possibility we next examine the specifics of recent deliveries of legal services. Has the client continued to receive value in the form of lower overall costs for legal services which are being delivered at premium prices?

4

The Decline of Cost-Effectiveness
Within the Large Law Firm

On the transformation of the highly specialized corporate law firm into the large law firm, the corporate law firm technique for delivering legal services at premium prices was extended to all areas of the firm's legal practice. Yet in many of these areas the technique provided few, if any, economic benefits to the client, either of scale or specialization. In those areas the client generally paid premium prices for average performance, in some instances premium prices for mediocre performance. But the large law firm possessed such prestige that clients remained indifferent to its charges, in the belief they were getting the best and nothing but the best would do. During the bonanza years of 1965 to 1990, these firms were able to set fees pretty much as they pleased, without fear of client displeasure or protest.

Misuse of the technique of specialization in fields where its use is inappropriate may be seen most clearly in trial practice. Basically, trial practice is one-on-one, one lawyer arguing to one judge, one lawyer examining one witness, one lawyer bearing responsibility for presentation of the case and for continuing evaluation of its tactics, strategy, and economics. Each case requires its own presentation and evaluation, in that formulaic precision and exactitude of outcome operate at a deep discount in trial work of any consequence. Each trial lawyer's style, preparation, and delivery are idiosyncratic. By reason of the greater number of variables inevitably associated with a trial routinization and formulation are not as useful as in corporate law work. The narrowness of sphere and subdivision of task employed so successfully in the corporate field can be an extravagance and a hindrance in the preparation and trial of a case in court. Subdivision of task may be particularly wasteful. In cases of some consequence it became habitual in many large law firms to routinely involve the services and fee charges of six to eight lawyers, who divide legal services on the basis of function: Lawyer A brings in the client; Lawyer B interviews the client, evaluates the claim, and charts a course of action; Lawyer C translates the client's claim into legal pleadings; Lawyer D investigates the facts and interviews witnesses to support the claim; Lawyer E conducts discovery (depositions, interrogatories, inspections, etc.) to establish a factual record for the claim and rebut potential defenses; Lawyer F tries the case in court, assisted by Lawyers G and H.

Alternatively, a firm may use multiple lawyers for different aspects of a case: Lawyer A deals with the client, Lawyer B tries the liability aspect of the case, Lawyer C tries the damage phase, Lawyer D examines and cross-examines expert witnesses, Lawyer E argues contested legal issues in court, and Lawyers F, G, and H assist the others in their presentations.

Each of these lawyers makes a record of his work so that the others may be kept informed. Periodic conferences among these lawyers are necessary so that all may know new developments in the case and thereby coordinate their activities. Each conference of lawyers and each review of interoffice memorandums about the case becomes a billable charge. As a result preparation for trial may involve services of six to eight lawyers instead of two or three. The client pays a premium price for each of their services, as if subdivision of task had produced a saving in costs. One example illustrates the cost of this duplication. In an extended hearing of a terminated chief executive officer's claim against his company for severance pay and benefits owed under his employment contract, the hearing was adjourned for one day to allow the claimant to consider a settlement offer. The offer was rejected, the claimant prevailed, and thereafter he sought reasonable attorneys' fees authorized under the contract. The fee application included an item of $16,600 in attorneys' fees on the day of consideration of the rejected settlement offer for the services of eight lawyers, who logged a total of 54 hours at an average charge in excess of $300 an hour.[1]

Patently, a six-pack system of handling litigation through the efforts of multiple lawyers, each dealing with a relatively small segment of the project, produces added costs. Yet excessive cost is not the only drawback of a multiple-lawyer system. The lawyer who tries the case in court may often not know it as well as he should and may not present it to best advantage because he relied too much on the work and impressions of others. He may not be wholly familiar with the issues and pleadings, he may not have met important witnesses until the day of trial, or he may not be fully prepared to adjust to the vagaries and unexpected developments of a trial. From time to time the spectacle unfolds of trial counsel stopping in the middle of his examination of a witness to fumble through papers beneath the counsel table, of counsel conducting an extended conference with his assistants while court and jury await, or, worse still, of an assistant tugging at counsel's sleeve to whisper a correction to some misstatement. In theory the six to eight lawyers function as a pack of trained Dobermans headed straight for the jugular. In practice they often resemble an assemblage of beagles milling in all directions to pick up a scent—any scent—worthy of noisy pursuit. This phenomenon of more being less may be observed in complicated trials involving the federal government, where, often as not, two lawyers on the government side run rings around a 12-pack of counsel on the other.

In short, the corporate law system that worked, and for complicated matters continues to work economically and profitably in certain specialized fields, is not generally transportable to trial work. The same may be said for such other fields of law as employment relations, intellectual property, will contests, and other areas of dispute not reducible to routinization and standardization. The factory system of production, which as developed by Frederick Taylor subdivides work into specific, repetitive movements, does not fit all areas of the law. Nevertheless, the large law firm embraced such a system for all its legal work and during the boom years of 1965 to 1990 succeeded in imposing premium fees for all types of legal business. The result was a level of fees that small law firms and sole practitioners promptly adopted as the standard for the profession. How did this come about and how could legal services remain overpriced for decades?

One explanation for this extension of premium prices to all types of legal services is found in the structure of the large law firm. Such a firm is staffed by a battalion of lawyers, all of comparable educational backgrounds and professional qualifications, whose principal surface varia tions are age and experience. Within the firm itself these lawyers are assigned to different legal duties, but all enjoy the prestige of affiliation with the firm. The relationship within the firm of those of comparable age and experience is one of equals. As in other large organizations, for example, the military, differences in responsibilities, skills, and pay are recognized, but these differences do not alter the basic equality of lawyers within the firm. This relationship requires that disparities in earnings not become sufficiently great to create an insurmountable gulf between lawyers of the same age and experience who perform different types of legal work for the firm.

In the transition of the corporate law firm to the full-service large law firm, relative compensation of lawyers within these firms evolved in the following manner. The trial lawyer in the firm believes he expends the same amount of toil and sweat in rendering legal services as does the corporate lawyer on the next floor, and therefore he is entitled to comparable compensation. He infers that his services are as valuable to the client as those of the corporate lawyer and therefore both should be similarly compensated. Since in our earlier hypothetical example the large law firm charges $1,250 for a day's work of the corporate lawyer, the trial lawyer concludes that a similar charge of $1,250 should be made for his day's work in court. On another floor the probate lawyer reaches the same conclusion about her charges, as does the real estate lawyer in another wing of the building. Thus, pressure arises for premium charges for all legal services performed by the large law firm. The path of least resistance is to so charge, which in fact is what happened. The vital link between superior product at a premium price and lower net cost to the client had been severed.

The effects of this change extended far beyond the large law firm and the fees it charged its own clients. To continue our hypothetical example, the individual or small-firm trial lawyer might originally charge $500 for a day's work in court. But he soon learns his opponent from the large law firm is charging $1,250 for the same day in court. Over time the solo trial lawyer, looking at performances in court, may see no discernible difference between the quality, quantity, and results of his work and those of the lawyer from the large law firm. The next development is not hard to predict. The individual or small-firm trial lawyer, having rightly or wrongly evaluated his work as on a par with that of the large firm trial lawyer, concludes he should charge similar fees for similar work. The result is that low-quality producers start to charge the same fees as high-quality producers. A new generally-quoted plateau of fees for legal services in court has been reached, which in short order becomes accepted as the prevailing standard. For purposes of general acceptance it does not greatly matter that the individual or small-firm lawyer may not always collect his premium fees and may not avoid discounting their amount. What does matter is that a new standard of fees for a day in court has been set. Under this norm all solvent clients now face premium fees for what may be average performance, fees often excessive in the light of the value of the services to the client and the stakes at risk.

In addition to premium prices for average performance, two other factors make the quality of legal services at the large law firm no longer what it once was. First is the previously-noted increase from 12 to 800 in the number of large law firms offering premium-priced legal services, each seeking to recruit the best and the brightest. But in any given generation the proportion of exceptionally-talented men and women remains more or less constant. With the exponential multiplication of the number of large law firms competing for their services, the pool of talented new lawyers becomes widely dispersed among firms.[2] With rare exceptions no one firm or group of firms today can show a demonstrable superiority in the potential of its recruits. Second, the general quality of legal education and legal training throughout the country has steadily improved during the past fifty years, resulting in a higher-quality average performance of legal services than in the past by better-educated and better-trained men and women. Thus, the leveling in quality comes from two directions, a leveling down within the large law firm and a leveling up in the legal profession as a whole.

We conclude that the extension of premium fees to all types of legal services is unjustified by any superiority of performance or results, and in many instances its only result is to increase client charges. How then could this situation have continued for decades?

5

The Magic of the Emperor's New Clothes Suspends the Law of Supply and Demand

The mechanism used to justify premium fees for all types of legal services delivered by large law firms is billable hours, whereby fees are calculated on the basis of time spent multiplied by the lawyer's hourly rate, the latter based on a lawyer's seniority and experience.

Once again, an evolutionary process is involved. Historically, a lawyer was paid a fee for each specific service—a pleading, a motion, an appearance in court, and so on. Fees were paid for specific acts, regardless of time spent in their performance. This scheme had the advantage of tying tangible services to specific payments, thereby enabling the client to see what services he was getting for his money. But it also had the disadvantage of encouraging useless and dilatory procedures that served the interest of the lawyer but not necessarily that of the client.

Paralleling and overlapping the fee-for-specific-service system was the flat fee, under which a lawyer was employed to handle a specific case or project for a fixed sum. The factors used to determine the amount of the flat fee were: (1) benefit of the services to the client and the amount of money involved; (2) difficulties of the work and the skills required; (3) anticipated time the work would take; and (4) experience and standing of counsel. The flat fee had the merit for the client of fixing in advance the cost of the services, but the demerit for the lawyer of occasional hardship resulting from unanticipated complexity and length of a problem. Meanwhile, lawyers began keeping records of work performed and time spent on specific projects in order to track the matters that occupied them and determine the comparative profitability of each activity.

Gradually, the importance in fee fixing of benefit to the client and difficulties of the work, diminished, and fees came to be based more and more on time spent and experience of counsel, the latter reflected in an hourly rate. Under this standard, fees were based on time spent on a client's affairs rather than value to the client of services performed. Differences in experience and standing of lawyers came to be stated in terms of charge per hour rather than amount of flat fee. In due course fees charged by the large law firm began to be calculated almost exclusively on the basis of hours spent multiplied by the hourly rate of the lawyer involved. Hourly billing and the use of computers provided a mechanical basis for determining amounts of fees. If a fee were challenged in court, its validity would be justified by evidence given by other lawyers that the time spent on the work was reasonable and that the hourly rate charged was the prevailing rate for lawyers of comparable experience and standing.

As a consequence of this method of calculating fees, routine or repetitive legal work performed by experienced lawyers commanded the same fees as the most difficult and exacting work, premium fees being charged the client in both instances. In time the gap between cost of legal services and benefit to client widened, so that in many instances a rational relationship between cost and benefit disappeared, for example a $100,000 fee to effect a $100,000 recovery. Under the billable-hours method of charging fees, the concept of fee for specific services all but disappeared, as did the understanding that a lawyer only earned fees for legal services and not for administrative, investigative, or clerical activities. Under the iron grip of billable hours, even the most trivial correspondence or telephone call or routine transmission of documents became billable time. Such a fixed, mechanical system, lacking outside controls, based exclusively on a lawyer's own calculations of his worth, his costs, and his time spent, is as susceptible to loose practices and abuses as any other system in which self-interest is not reined in by outside review.

In establishing billable hours and hourly rates as the standard method for calculating fees, the large law firm succeeded in marketing its services on what amounted to a cost-plus basis, with both the cost factor and the plus factor selected by the firm itself. The result was a sale of services under which, as in government cost-plus contracts, the more time spent performing the services and the more personnel used on a given project, the greater the fee. We have a classic instance of the operation of Parkinson's Law: Work expands to fill the time available, time spent swells the importance of the work, and both escalate fees. Calculation of fees at hourly rates resembles a taxi meter operating on time alone—with distance traveled to destination immaterial.

To illustrate the effect of these changes we return to our hypothetical example of the cost of the now-routine task of incorporating a Delaware corporation. For reasons mentioned earlier, the average quality of the work done in the large law firm as successor to the corporate law firm, has receded toward the median and its cost-effectiveness has been weakened by the system of billable hours. The project is now one of 2.5 hours, for which a charge of $250 an hour is made for a total cost to the client of $625. Meanwhile, the individual practitioner takes the same five hours and charges the same $500. Thus for the same corporate service the work of the large law firm has become more expensive than that of the individual practitioner and the possibility that it will be conspicuously superior has narrowed. But the matter does not rest there. The individual practitioner, concluding that the quality of his work is equal to that of the large law firm and that he should be compensated accordingly, soon raises his fee to $625 in order to charge what he perceives to be the prevailing rate for such a service. The result is that the client pays considerably more than it formerly did for the identical service. The great merit of the corporate law firm that enabled it to deliver for a premium fee a superior product at a cheaper cost to the client has been lost in the endless corridors of the large law firm.

Still, the puzzle remains. Why does the vendor of legal services call the tune and not the purchaser? Why are fees charged on a cost basis and not a competitive basis? Why are fees up instead of down, as we might expect from the exponential increase in the availability of large law firms as suppliers of legal services? There are several reasons.

PRESTIGE

The great prestige of the corporate law firm remained intact on its evolution into the large law firm. Until recently clients remained willing to pay premium prices for all types of services when performed by a large law firm as successor to the corporate law firm. Premium fees deservedly earned for complicated corporate work were carried over to all fees of the firm on its evolution into the large law firm engaged in all types of practice.

Other, newly-organized, large law firms emulated the methods of the earlier corporate law firms, and did it so successfully that it soon became difficult to differentiate between the older and the newer large law firms. On the basis of size alone these newer firms were able to conjure up prestige comparable to that earned over the years by the old firms, on the strength of which they, too, were able to charge premium prices for the entire range of legal services. In this activity, the key factors were inculcation and cultivation of the beliefs that size equals quality, that bigger is better, and that subdivision of task is cost-effective for all types of law work. Cultivation of these beliefs was fortified by an argument taken from the luxury-goods trade: Premium prices assure quality, and a low-priced lawyer necessarily cannot be as skilled as a lawyer who charges premium prices. The combination of these two beliefs—bigger is better, and high price assures high quality—acclimated clients of both old and new large law firms to pay premium prices for the entire range of legal services.

DIFFICULTY IN LAY EVALUATION OF LEGAL SERVICES

The factor of prestige can dominate indefinitely, even in the face of contrary evidence, so long as a client has no effective way to evaluate the relative merit and cost of the legal services he receives and compare them with what he might get elsewhere. The services are intangible. Their extent and ultimate worth cannot readily be determined in that the variables connected with legal services admit unending analysis and interpretation. Moreover, the mystique of legal practice is available to experienced seniors in large law firms to convince a client who questions fees that the client's view of legal matters is incomplete, that the procedures undertaken and costs incurred in a particular project are essential for its proper disposition, that unless the firm is permitted to handle matters its own way it cannot take responsibility for the project's final outcome. Normally, one such session brings the client to heel and allays whatever reservations he may have felt about premium fees. The greater the prestige of the firm, the more likely this will be the outcome. In such fashion pricing of legal services, as noted by Guy Rounsaville, general counsel of Wells Fargo Bank, remains as much a black box mystery as the pricing of modern art.[1]

A further difficulty in client evaluation of the cost-effectiveness of legal services arises when the services are rendered over a period of years. The ultimate cost of the project may be unforeseeable, no particular step may appear decisive, and no single cost may appear excessive. Only after the matter has been concluded, perhaps years later, can cost-effectiveness be evaluated.

SAFETY

Purchasers of mainstream legal services are usually acting in a representative and not a personal capacity. The purchasing agent, more often than not, has someone looking over his shoulder for mishaps or errors of judgment. When he undertakes to employ counsel, an important consideration in his mind is the safety of his own position, that is, that he cannot be faulted later for his selection or continued use of specific counsel. In turning to the large law firm for specific services, he has reasonable assurance that the services will be performed with at least average competency. If he goes elsewhere, even when he has information that a smaller vendor of legal services is equally competent and can supply the identical services at lower cost, he runs a greater risk of criticism should the outcome prove disappointing. Why chance it? The safer course, therefore, is to employ the large law firm for all work, even when this involves payment of premium prices for work that is routine. In view of the greater risk of criticism if something should go awry, representation by a prestigious law firm often outweighs any desire for cost-effectiveness. Thus the dominance of the large law firm continues, regardless of cost.

Selection of legal-service providers is comparable to the casting of a play. A producer wants the security of experienced actors of known quality. The only way actors can acquire experience is to be hired by producers. Thus, the same actors continue as leads year after year. So it is with employment of law firms. The operation of this safety principle in the legal world can be seen in the employment of municipal bond counsel to provide an opinion on the validity of bonds to be issued by a public entity. Many lawyers are capable of doing this work, but in any given locality the work gravitates to a tiny handful of law firms. For instance, Orrick Herrington (San Francisco) has dominated this business in northern California for the past 60 years. Other lawyers, perhaps even former members of this firm, are capable of doing this work. Nevertheless, public authorities in large part continue to employ the same firm,[2] because, it is said, the underwriters who purchase the bonds for resale to the ultimate buyers insist on an opinion vouching for the validity of the bonds from a well-known law firm, and might, it is thought, decline to underwrite a bond issue if another lawyer or law firm were opining on the bonds' validity. Hence, year after year, regardless of cost, this type of legal business remains for the most part in the same hands, the factor of reputation superseding considerations of expense.

One aspect of safety is preservation of a client's confidences—its trade secrets, its business plans for expansion or contraction, its finances, its vulnerabilities. A client that has had a good relationship with a specific law firm for years or decades may place well-warranted confidence in the discretion and integrity of that firm, and be reluctant to disclose important confidences to other lawyers with whom it has not had past dealings and about whose discretion it has no knowledge. At times this factor may overrule all others, including costs—and rightly so for critical issues—but it has little application to routine legal matters in which confidentiality is no great matter.

INERTIA

Closely allied to safety is the factor of consumer inertia, which embraces the comfort of a familiar product and resists any change requiring an outlay of time and effort that might be spent more profitably on other matters. As consumers we buy soap and toothpaste, coffee and tea, television sets and refrigerators under brand or trade names. Because the name gives us an assurance of average quality and average reliability and saves us the time and trouble of evaluating unknown products, we are willing to pay a somewhat higher price. It is the same with services, where we may continue to employ the electrician or plumber we know, even though his charges are higher than others. Similar considerations apply to procurement of legal services. Until recently legal costs of a business client constituted a relatively small proportion of its cost of doing business. A client was apt to conclude it should stay with a familiar law firm even though the costs of the firm's services were higher than might be found elsewhere. The spectacular increases in the size of legal fees that occurred in the 1960s, '70s, and '80s were in large part a product of this client inertia.

But as legal costs continued to rise as a proportion of the cost of doing business, the importance of the inertia factor declined. In the same manner that we as householders become more cost-conscious when faced with such major expenditures as a new electrical system or a new plumbing system, so clients pay greater attention to the costs of legal services as they rise.

CAPTIVE CLIENTS

A corporate client's board of directors frequently includes a member of the law firm that is its chief provider of legal services. In these instances the law firm is in a preferred position to obtain all major legal work of that corporation and, absent gross discrepancies in costs, to continue to monopolize such work. In such corporations the general counsel may be a minor figure within the corporate hierarchy in no position to cavil over fees submitted by a law firm whose member sits on his board of directors. The consequence may be that the corporate client pays all the law firm's fees with little or no review and without arms-length bargaining. A comparable result may follow when the general counsel was formerly employed by the law firm doing the corporation's legal work and had secured his present position through the blessing of his former firm. It is unlikely that a general counsel who owes his position to the sponsorship of the law firm will engage in hard bargaining over his former firm's fees. These special relationships are not limited to large or medium-size corporations, but may also be found in smaller enterprises, in real estate partnerships, in trust relationships, banking relationships, and political relationships. Each special or sweet-heart relationship offers an opportunity to keep legal fees artificially high, which in turn establishes a benchmark that sets the prevailing standard of fees for similar services.

ABSENCE OF EXTERNAL STANDARDS AND CONTROLS

Lawyers have been given a monopoly of appearances in court on be-half of others, and this monopoly extends to the rendering of legal advice about litigation and about the legal validity of documents. Ostensibly this monopoly is tolerable because it is regulated by guilds (bar asso-ciations) and by courts.

But as noted earlier, the effectiveness of lawyer regulation by bar as-sociations has weakened. Like other trade groups, bar associations are primarily concerned with professional problems affecting the welfare of their members and have shown little consistent interest in limiting the fees its members charge. In past years bar associations were active in promulgating minimum fee schedules that have since been discredited as illegal restraints of trade[3]; in restricting nonresident lawyers from the practice of law in a given state, a restriction ruled invalid by the Supreme Court in 1985[4]; in attempting to monopolize for lawyers appearances before administrative agencies; and in preventing banks, accountants, tax consultants, and estate planners from invading turf the lawyers con-sider their own.[5] Bar associations are currently active in conducting public relations campaigns to improve the public image of lawyers, an exercise in futility because, in Professor Abel's words, "lawyers must change who they are and what they do" if they wish to modify their public perception as hired guns.[6] Aside from periodic proclamation of abstract standards for the determination of reasonable fees (of which more later) bar associations have done little to curb excessive fees, their efforts in this area rarely extending beyond instances of demonstrable lawyer fraud or theft. Timidity and halfheartedness are the hallmarks of reform from within. For example, in December 1993 the ethics com-mittee of the American Bar Association promulgated a ruling that law-yers should not bill two clients for the same hours or bill more time on a matter than is actually spent.[7]

Bar associations have been further weakened by the loss of some of their most important functions, such as conduct of disbarment pro-ceedings, investigation of judicial misconduct, and recommendations for improvement in law administration. To an increasing extent, these functions are being transferred to government institutions with full-time staffs.[8] As a consequence of these losses, participation in bar association activities by leaders of the profession has declined, thereby further reducing the effectiveness of these organizations as instruments of independent control over lawyer conduct.

Until recent years a similar timidity characterized state legislatures and Congress, whose members in large part have been lawyers whose primary sympathies tended more toward their fellow lawyers than toward clients. A few statutory controls over fees exist in specific fields of legal work—for example, in probate proceedings and collection of debts (subject, however, to added fees for extraordinary services)—but by and large, legislatures have left controls over fees to the discretion of the courts. Ostensibly courts are in a position to control excessive legal fees of the lawyers they have admitted to practice and over whose conduct they exercise disciplinary powers, including that of disbarment. But in fact once a lawyer has been admitted to practice, court control over his activities, other than palpable misconduct, becomes virtually nonexistent. With rare exceptions—guardianship, contracts of minors, contracts of incompetents—lawyers are free to make fee arrangements with clients on any mutually agreed terms, and for reasons discussed later courts have been content to let lawyers set standards of reasonableness for fees.

In sum, legal fees are fixed almost exclusively by lawyers themselves. Were the situation reversed—were a group of clients or expert laywitnesses with client experience asked to set fees—the level of reasonable fees would surely be lower. But under present practices the lawyers' monopoly of appearance in court extends in effect to a monopoly over determination of reasonableness of fees. As long as this condition exists, the focus in fee disputes in court is apt to center on the well-being of the lawyer, less so on that of the client.

The several factors bringing about toleration of premium fees reinforce one another to produce a general acceptance of premium fees. Nevertheless, fees can escalate even above premium levels and become grossly excessive when abusive practices are tolerated. Some of these abusive practices are set out in the next chapter.

6

Excessive Legal Fees: The Count Dracula Clients Cannot Stake

We have seen premium fees spread to all types of legal activity and their use continue more or less unchallenged. The professional motivation for lawyers to deliver the best possible service to their clients at the lowest cost now competes with a pernicious motivation inherent in hourly billings, under which the more time spent on a project, the greater the fee.[1] Use of the billing system that has prevailed since 1965 puts client and lawyer in an adversarial relationship, in that the interest of the client favors expeditious and economical disposition of a matter while that of the lawyer favors comprehensive and exhaustive disposition. As a consequence premium fees often become excessive fees. This does not occur in all law firms, nor does it involve all lawyers in law firms in which it does occur. But it happens more often than it should.

The mechanics that produce excessive fees include one or more inherently abusive practices.[2]

OVERSTAFFING

The most persistent abuse is overstaffing, in which, as discussed earlier, six to eight lawyers are employed on a matter where two or three would suffice. Overstaffing may also result from lack of continuity in employment of lawyers on a project when the law firm's interest in re-deployment of its personnel takes precedence over the client's interest in continuity of counsel. Substitutions may result in substantial hourly billings for time spent by new personnel learning what their predecessors knew. An example is a single-site environmental pollution case in which during a period of three years 47 lawyers from the same law firm worked for the same client on that one case.[3]

An incentive for overstaffing can be found in leverage, the practice under which senior lawyers who own the law firm charge a client more than the firm's actual expenses for the legal services of juniors who work on the client's affairs. To hypothesize, if the cost to the law firm of a junior is $120,000 a year ($80,000 salary and $40,000 overhead) and the law firm can collect $220,000 from clients for the junior's services (2,000 billable hours at $110 an hour) it will make $100,000 profit in addition to the profits earned from fees for the services of the seniors themselves. In theory, the greater the number of juniors thus employed, the greater the profits that will accrue to the seniors. In short, leverage is a practical application of the nineteenth-century theory of the surplus value of labor. Leverage at its best has been described by John P. Quinn of Price Waterhouse in his book *Law Firm Accounting*: "Partner leverage represents the law firm partners' ability to provide quality service to clients, in a timely manner, while delegating the bulk of the work to associates for completion."[4] The profitability of leverage in actual practice is difficult to determine, since no public accountings of law firm receipts and expenses are available and lawyers have no desire to educate clients on law firm profit margins. But the profession believes leverage to be a significant factor in increasing profits, and belief alone may produce a benign view of overstaffing. Yet if the law firm's business remains static (that is, if it consists of the same clients with the same volume of legal activity as in the previous year), leveraged profits may be impossible to sustain as a consequence of promotion of juniors to seniors or of employment of juniors for whom there is insufficient work. To illustrate, when a junior is promoted to senior, the change requires employment of more juniors to maintain the same ratio of leverage. Thus if a firm of 150 lawyers (100 juniors, 50 seniors) promotes a junior to senior status, it will need to hire three additional juniors and become a firm of 153 lawyers to preserve its two-to-one leverage ratio. It must also find additional business to keep its larger number of lawyers busy. Accordingly, to keep leveraged profits in good health, a firm may need constant increases in the size of its billings,[5] absent which a continuing temptation exists to indulge in legal featherbedding by assigning four lawyers to do the work of two and billing accordingly.

OVERLOADING

Overloading duplicates some of the ground found in overstaffing but possesses its own twists. We identify overloading as the performance of services of no real value to the client. A law suit may be filed when settlement of a dispute is reasonably certain. The full panoply of discovery may be unleashed, even though the essential facts are already known. Supplemental pleadings may be added, motions made, new parties brought in, provisional remedies sought—all to gain doubtful advantage under the rationale that zealous advocacy compels such activities. Too often the sole result of such a hurricane of activity is a flood of hourly billings.

Overloading may also result when a long, complicated, continuing matter of no specific urgency or set determination is pending in the large law firm and serves as a cash cow that junior and senior lawyers alike can milk on a slow day or when hourly billings need augmentation to maintain status within the firm. Such sporadic work may amount to no more than a reshuffle of existing papers, a recollection of thoughts formulated earlier, to be forgotten again in the absence of continuous effort. The client, however, is billed as through this work of recall at irregular intervals was of real benefit to him.

In sum, overloading bears an uncomfortable resemblance to a stockbroker's churning an unrestricted investment account.

OVERQUALIFYING

Overqualifying involves performance by a senior of routine legal, investigative, or organizational services for which the lawyer is overqualified but for which the client is billed at full premium rates. In such instances the client pays premium hourly rates, justifiable only for the performance of highly-skilled legal services, when in fact the services are those a junior, a paralegal, or a secretary could perform with equal competence. Overqualifying may result when a senior lawyer, facing a slow afternoon, spends three hours reorganizing, regrouping, and reclassifying papers in a sprawling file that has outgrown its initial organization. A necessary task? Yes, but not at a cost to the client of $300 an hour. In 15 minutes the senior can instruct his secretary or a paralegal how he wants the file reorganized and thereafter bill his client for 15 minutes of his time rather than three hours. Such overqualification is most common in a law firm that is top-heavy with seniors who need to keep occupied. It may extend down the chain of responsibility, so that junior lawyers regularly do work that could be done by paralegals or investigators, paralegals do work that could be done by legal secretaries, and legal secretaries do work that could be done by filing clerks.

The paradox of overqualifying is that, like overstaffing, it not only results in extra cost to the client, but in many instances produces inferior work. For example, investigation is a highly-skilled art that requires training in specific techniques and demands extensive and exact knowledge of the sources, availability, and reliability of specific information essential to the investigation. Specially trained agents, such as those of the Federal Bureau of Investigation and the Internal Revenue Service, can produce information from sources that would not occur to an untrained investigator, can weigh and evaluate leads that unearth critical facts, and can organize masses of facts into readily comprehensible and usable form. Ordinarily, a junior lawyer in a large law firm has had no investigative training, and the investigative results of such a lawyer, for whose services the client is charged full legal rates, are frequently inferior to those a trained investigator could have obtained at a lesser cost to the client.

OVERBILLING

Under the system of billable hours, time spent on a client's affairs is calculated in quarter-hour or tenth-of-hour segments. Each lawyer logs her day's work, indicating the clients for whom she worked, how long she worked, and what services she performed. The log becomes part of the firm's permanent records, used to bill clients and to evaluate productivity and profitability of each lawyer in the firm. At one time 1,500 billable hours a year (roughly 30 hours a week for 50 weeks) was considered the norm for a working lawyer. In recent years this norm has increased to 1,800 to 2,000 hours, at some law firms even to 2,200 to 2,400 billable hours as a goal. To what extent are these hourly increases realistic? The rationale for use of premium rates to calculate fees assumes a lawyer is working on her client's affairs at optimum capacity and at her highest level of professional competence throughout the billed period, much as a surgeon works while in the operating theatre, and therefore hourly charges of $150 to $500 are justifiable. Hence the subdivision of billable hours into fifteen-minute or six-minute segments to ensure full value to the client for every fraction of an hour charged.

But consider other demands on a lawyer's time, demands that must be met if she is to function at highest capacity on behalf of her clients. Some of these demands occur daily, some at regular intervals, and some episodically throughout the year. If we apportion these various demands to each working day, we can estimate how much of the day's time they occupy. Assume a lawyer is at work every day for nine hours from 9 A.M. to 6 P.M. From these nine hours the following time must be subtracted:

Lunch	1 hour
Personal hygiene	¼ hour
Secretarial-clerical dealings	¼ hour
Dealings with colleagues	¼ hour
Current professional literature	¼ hour
Personal affairs	¼ hour
New business possibilities	¼ hour
Pro bono service	¼ hour
Civic and bar association activity	¼ hour
Wasted time	0
Total	3 hours

Thus in an average nine-hour day, a third of the lawyer's time is taken up by other demands on her attention, leaving only six hours available for billing purposes, a ratio still considerably better than that of the one-hour football game that takes three hours to play. While some of these demands may be postponed temporarily, the demands themselves remain inflexible and must be satisfied at one time or another during the year if the lawyer is to continue as one fully qualified to charge premium fees.

Our 9-to-6 lawyer thus will produce, on average, six billable hours during her nine hours at work, 30 billable hours during a five-day week and 1,500 billable hours during a 50-week year. If under the same conditions she works every Saturday and ignores the ten federal holidays, she will produce thirty-six billable hours weekly and 1,800 billable hours yearly, a figure now viewed as the norm. If she extends her time at work from 9 A.M. to 7 P.M., works six days a week, ignores all holidays, and does this 50 weeks a year, she will log 40 billable hours weekly for a total of 2,000 hours yearly.

Beyond these numbers we enter the realm of fantasy, one in which for hourly billing purposes a lawyer is depicted as a kind of zombie or robot programmed to function at optimum capacity day and night solely and exclusively on client affairs. This depiction is what lawyers call a legal fiction—a state of affairs contrary to fact but one the lawyer assumes to be true. Although it is fact that a lawyer can put in great numbers of hours at his workplace, and log 2,200 or 2,400 hours yearly, it is also fact that he cannot do so at the optimum capacity and at the highest level of professional competence that provides the sole justification for premium hourly rates, any more than could the operating surgeon. While under extraordinary circumstances and for brief periods of a day, a week, even a month, a lawyer may be capable of functioning at top capability around the clock, he cannot do so without corresponding periods of rest and attention to other demands on his time. Neither can he continue to do so month after month, year after year, as billings of 2,200 or 2,400 hours a year imply.

What has happened is that calculation now works backwards. At the end of a 9-to-6 day, the lawyer who has been busy all day undertakes to record his billable hours. Subtracting an hour for lunch (if he went out), he apportions the remaining eight hours among the clients on whose affairs he worked that day. Ignored or forgotten are those other demands on his time that required his attention during the day. In such fashion a five-day week produces without undue sweat a weekly harvest of 40 billable hours, and a 50-week year one of 2,000 billable hours. This development may be described as the new math. Under its operation 1,500 billable hours yearly have increased to 2,000 hours yearly with no real change in the amount of work done or the time spent doing it. Time has been synthesized into a higher stage of truth whose verisimilitude is corroborated by the artistic pledge of billings in six-minute segments.

OVERACHIEVING

Overachieving is a byproduct of the effect of leverage on the promotion process. As discussed earlier, the large law firm is organized to allow its seniors to make a profit by marketing the legal services of its juniors. Normally, the greater the volume of these services and the higher the ratio of juniors to seniors, the greater the profits that will accrue to the seniors. As a consequence promotions from junior to senior status are made only to fill specific firm needs, such as replacement of depleted ranks of seniors, retention of a key junior who threatens to leave, or stimulation of recruitment of beginning lawyers. Under such a regime only a small minority of juniors in a large law firm ever achieves senior status, with the result that competition among juniors for preferment is intense, often resembling the struggle for the remaining seats on the last helicopter out of Saigon. An important factor in this competition is the number of billable hours logged yearly by a junior, who is directly or tacitly encouraged to work long hours and who receives firm approbation for so doing. Hence it is not surprising that some juniors are eager to exploit all possibilities of extracting billable hours from matters to which they have been assigned. A regime in which a junior's professional advancement is linked to billable hours presents a continuing temptation for the junior to magnify his hours. In addition to generous estimates of the passage of time, magnification may include performance of marginal services, duplicative services, or even useless services under the pretext that something new might turn up. When one junior overreports, other juniors competing for promotion are tempted to do likewise, under the rationalization that they are merely evening up the competition. If seniors turn a blind eye to overachievement, what started as a lapse by one junior may become habitual for all, and fees in such a firm may become chronically excessive.

OVERTRYING

In a trial, lawyers who are paid under a system of hourly rates have a financial interest in the length of the cause, in that the longer it lasts the larger their fees. Here, too, temptation arises to perform marginal or duplicative services, to call witnesses of little real value, and to argue every point at length, all under the banner of thoroughness and zealous representation. Once again the paradox arises that more may be less, that excessive amounts of time spent on a given presentation, cross-examination, or argumentation can produce a poorer result than shorter, more focused, and more incisive treatment. If too many witnesses, too much evidence, too many arguments, and too many exhibits are introduced, such overkill obscures and detracts from the basic facts and issues of the case, makes what should be clear unclear, what should be certain uncertain, and what should be incisive diffuse. It may produce doubts in the mind of the judge and jury where none should exist. Thus overtrying is doubly hurtful to the client, because in addition to added expense it can adversely affect the outcome of the case.

On occasion, lawyers on both sides of a cause overtry their cases, both being employed by solvent clients at hourly rates and neither having any incentive to bring about a speedy conclusion. In a recent contract cause plaintiffs secured judgment for $1.9 million but paid out $1.9 million for legal fees and costs while defendants paid out $3.9 million for legal fees and costs, for total legal expenses of $5.8 million, more than three times the amount of the judgment. Patently, the sole real beneficiaries of the litigation were the lawyers.[6]

PROFIT CENTERS

The idea has spread among large law firms that each administrative activity within the firm should produce a profit over and above that earned by lawyers for performing legal services. In many firms the use of hourly charges has been extended to the work of paralegals, secretaries, librarians, word processors, photocopiers, messengers, clerical assemblers, and other employees whose services are used in handling a client's affairs. Charges to the client may include use of electronic legal research equipment, rent for use of the law firm's own conference rooms, and catering of coffee and Danish for conferences. Sometimes client billings obscure the nature of these overhead charges, as in items labeled HVAC, which, when decoded, refer to office heat, ventilation, and air conditioning turned on by a lawyer working on a weekend.[7] Under the profit-center concept each activity involving goods or services used in rendering legal services to the client must produce a profit of its own.

What has happened is that an increasing proportion of a law firm's overhead—rent, secretarial overtime, library expense, postage, communications, document preparation, document delivery—is being transformed into direct charges billed to the client. Formerly, a lawyer's overhead was his own responsibility, paid by him out of fees received. Today massive amounts of overhead are charged to the client as direct costs, and these costs may carry an undisclosed markup designed to make a profit for the law firm. In this activity, named *Skaddenomics* after its most diligent practitioner, the lawyer functions as businessman, akin to a building contractor who obtains materials, recruits carpenters, plumbers, electricians, and other artisans, and collects payment for these materials and services from the owner at a percentage markup above amounts paid out, thus securing a profit for himself as entrepreneur. Most large law firms soon followed the lead of Skadden Arps.[8] The former managing partner of Latham & Watkins, the second-largest Los Angeles law firm at the time, has been quoted as blaming New York firms for starting these practices but declaring his firm "saw the trend and felt we had to follow or we'd be leaving money on the table."[9]

Where the large law firm leads, the small law firm is happy to follow, in some instances with none of the institutional restraint that moderates the large law firm's markups. Absent effective client control, some of these markups are spectacular. For example, photostatic copies of documents have been charged to the client at a dollar a page when the actual cost to the lawyer may have been as little as five cents. In a suit involving a $6 million recovery, $1 million was collected by plaintiffs' lawyer for photocopying at a dollar a page.[10] More customary are photocopying charges of 25 cents a page for services whose direct cost may be ten cents a page. The photocopier—a profit center for lawyers.

FRAUD

The relative concept of time produced by a system of billable hours that has lost touch with finite and tangible measurement fosters a moral elasticity among users of the system that on occasion stretches into sharp practice and misrepresentation amounting to fraud. Billable hours may and have produced 27-hour days. Two or more clients may be billed for the same court appearance. A lawyer on a transcontinental flight may simultaneously bill client A for four hours of travel time and client B for four hours of legal research. For one day's service in an asbestos cause a lawyer reportedly billed 5,000 clients for two-tenths of an hour each, thus producing what may be the first 1,000-hour day.[11] Clients may be billed for time spent on legal research in another case involving similar legal points, a practice known as phantom-hour billing. Under such a billing the client pays for expertise twice, once at the lawyer's high hourly rate and again by way of phantom hours. A 15-minute court appearance may be billed as one of three hours. Computers may be programmed or billing clerks instructed to automatically increase all time records by 15 percent.[12] A lawyer may bill for time spent commuting between home and office. The fine line between billable hours as a relative concept of time and actual fraud is being crossed with growing frequency, the pretext being that the lawyer is thinking of his client's affairs every waking hour—on occasion even dreaming of them in his sleep. Whether fraud in billing practices leads to a higher incidence of fraud in other matters remains an open question best left to philosophers, psychiatrists, and theologians.

It must be emphasized again that not all law firms and not all lawyers indulge in these practices. Yet the practices have become sufficiently widespread to achieve a degree of toleration throughout the profession, rationalized by the comforting conclusion that it is the responsibility of the client to control excessive fees. But what of the courts? Are they not obligated to control excessive fees and discipline fee abusers, whether individual lawyers or firms?

7

Excessive Legal Fees: Even the Courts Can't Stake Dracula

We have seen briefly that courts have generally left the subject of legal fees to lawyers. Yet because the privileged status given lawyers by the courts is also revocable by the courts, we must explain why courts have been unable and unwilling to exercise effective control over legal fees that are excessive. In certain instances judges are required to set legal fees, for example, when lawyers and clients take their fee disputes to court, when a contract or statute requires the losing litigant to pay the winner's legal fees, or when a class suit creates a common fund from which legal fees are to be awarded. Although these instances constitute only a small fraction of total legal fees, why don't the courts in these cases establish standards that make reasonable fees the norm and premium or excessive fees the exception?

Several factors militate against effective court control of legal fees.

RELATIVE WEAKNESS OF JUDGES

In this country there are over 800,000 lawyers and perhaps 20,000 full-time judges. Lawyers and lawyers' lobbies are powerful in Congress and in every state legislature. Lawyers occupy positions of prestige in all types of public and private organizations, and they largely monopolize political and campaign activities. Conversely, judges are few in numbers and speak only sporadically as an organized group. They are precluded from lobbying and political activity, and are discouraged from serving in public or private positions of influence outside the judicial posts they hold. The judicial world is largely an artificial, reactive world in which the judge remains a step removed from actual events. The consequent disparity in power and influence between the two groups is striking. On the sensitive subject of legal fees, the interest of lawyers is direct and concrete while that of judges is peripheral and abstract, and it begs human experience to expect a weak group to take arms against the strong on a subject academic to the weak but central to the strong. In addition, the judge as a former lawyer remains sensitive to the basic interests of the legal profession even after ascending the bench. This sensitivity on the part of the judge reflects a degree of self-interest, for a judge who embarks on a crusade that antagonizes influential members of the bar may find himself in trouble when re-election, reappointment, or promotion comes up and he needs the support of the bar.

STANDARDS FOR LEGAL FEES REMAIN THE PROVINCE OF LAWYERS

On those occasions when judges do set fees, they are required to set them under a standard of prevailing charges for similar legal services, and prevailing charges are proved by the testimony of lawyers. Because lawyers are the ones who both set and bear witness to prevailing levels of fees, the process regularly results in approval of premium fees that reflect full solicitude for the welfare of the legal profession. In short, the standard is tailored to the interests of lawyers and not those of clients.

To alleviate the frustration of conscientious judges brought on by their inability to exercise any real control over premium or excessive fees, elaborate rituals have grown up. For example, a law firm seeking a $2 million fee for services in a common-fund cause will prepare a fee application outlining all work that might have some conceivable relationship to the case, translate this product into terms of generous hours at generous hourly rates, and present a fee application for $3 million, 50 percent above what it hopes to get. In support of its application it confronts the court with a monumental mass of paperwork and timesheets and the testimony of lawyers as expert witnesses averring the reasonableness of the fees and the necessity for all services performed. The judge may feel frustrated by the mass of data supporting the fee application and by the absence or sketchiness of any contrary evidence. But if inclined to take action, he or she will undertake a superficial review of the application, locate obvious holes and duplications in the supporting data, and then triumphantly reduce the application by a third, from $3 million to $2 million, the latter being the sum the applicant firm planned to get in the first place.[1] Under this stylized kabuki the law firm collects its premium fees, the judge acquires a reputation for vigilance in the public interest, and only the clients lose out. In point of fact no effective control over the fee has been exercised.

A second ritual involves an endless expansion in the number of factors used as standards for determining reasonableness of legal fees. These solemn formulations have reached a point of inanity insofar as they undertake to furnish any practical basis for determining reasonableness. It is instructive to summarize the evolution of the formulations created by lawyers and then adopted by courts.

A starting point is *Stanton v. Embrey*, an 1876 Supreme Court case discussing the amount of fees properly chargeable for legal services.[2] Reasonable fees, said the court, are determined by the nature of the services and the lawyer's standing in the profession for skill and proficiency, which may be proved by testimony of other lawyers stating the usual charges for similar services by lawyers of comparable standing. The case thus sets out two factors for determining reasonableness of fees: (1) the nature of the services; and (2) the skill and proficiency of the lawyer rendering the services. Additionally, it approved use of lawyers as expert witnesses on customary charges.

But from this simple rule of determining reasonableness of fees on the basis of two factors—nature of the services and standing of the lawyer—the criteria have steadily multiplied. By 1931 there were six factors to be considered by the courts in evaluating fees.[3] Factor inflation continued, until in 1974 in the leading case of *Johnson v. Georgia Highway Express Inc.*,[4] relevant factors had grown to twelve, factors directly taken from the American Bar Association's Code of Professional Responsibility, Disciplinary Rule 2–106.

As set out in *Johnson*, these factors are:

1. The time and labor required
2. The novelty and difficulty of the questions
3. The skill requisite to perform the legal service properly
4. The preclusion of employment by the attorney due to acceptance of the case
5. The customary fee
6. Whether the fee is fixed or contingent
7. Time limitations imposed by the client or the circumstances
8. The amount involved and the results obtained
9. The experience, reputation, and ability of the attorneys
10. The "undesirability" of the case

11. The nature and length of the professional relationship with the client

12. Awards in similar cases.

In 1983 these 12 factors received the stamp of approval from the Supreme Court in *Hensley v. Eckerhart*,[5] over a dissent by one justice who argued that even more factors should be considered, principally increased fees for contingent-fee cases in order to cover losses in other cases that produced no fee. Formulation of comparable multifactored tests is widespread among bar associations. For example, the State Bar of California itemizes 11 items as "among the factors to be considered" in determining unconscionability of a fee.[6]

Recent rulings by the courts on reasonableness of fees have almost unanimously adopted as the basic standard for fees time spent on the matter multiplied by an hourly rate, stating that reasonable hours at a reasonable rate make a reasonable fee. This figure is known as the lodestar fee. Its amount may then be adjusted up depending on the contingency of success and the quality of a lawyer's work, a process known as enhancement. In 1986 the Supreme Court in *Pennsylvania v. Delaware Citizens Council*[7] discussed but did not decide the propriety of enhancement of lodestar fees for success in contingent fee cases, over the dissent of three justices who supported the trial judge's use of contingency-fee multipliers of two and four for work in certain phases of the litigation.

In 1992 lodestar enhancement of fees again came before the Supreme Court in *City of Burlington v. Dague*,[8] in which the court rejected enhancement, holding that reasonable hours at a reasonable rate constitutes a reasonable fee, that enhancement for contingency would require clients bringing meritorious cases to subsidize clients bringing losing cases. Three justices dissented, arguing that without a multiplier, competent lawyers would not be attracted to contingency litigation. It is difficult to tell whether enhancement of lodestar fees is dead or merely asleep in a cave awaiting the call of Roland's horn. What is clear is that hours spent times lawyer rate is prima facie evidence of a reasonable fee, one on which pressure to adjust is almost invariably up, not down. It is equally clear that a standard for determining reasonableness of fees that relies on 12 variables whose relative proportions are subject to evaluation in each case constitutes no standard at all. Of the 12 factors currently itemized, only the eighth, the amount involved and the results obtained, considers reasonableness of fees from the viewpoint of the client. All others look at fees from the lawyer's perspective.

In point of fact, reasonable fees are a function of two elements: (1) value of the services to the client; and (2) lawyer willingness to undertake the engagement. If courts are required to fix fees exclusively on the basis of the second factor, as made concrete by lawyer representations of prevailing charges for the engagement, there is little courts can do to bring about reasonableness of fees during a period of sustained fee inflation. In sum, on issues of reasonableness of fees courts have played a peripheral role and have possessed neither the incentive nor the tools to become agents of change. Court acceptance of fees based on a lawyer's report of time spent multiplied by the lawyer's self-determined hourly rate and validated as prevailing charges has become well-nigh universal. Like stock market prices in a sustained boom, prevailing charges for legal services can continue overpriced for years.

SUMMARY

To illustrate the inadequacy of controls over legal fees, we can imagine a comparable system in place for settling disputes over plumbing bills that have been computed at the plumber's hourly rate, with time spent determined exclusively by the plumber's own time reports. Under this system, a customer protesting a bill would have the right to demand a hearing before a Bureau of Plumbers, where testimony as to reasonableness of charges would be given exclusively by other plumbers, on the basis of standards for charges adopted by the Plumbers Trade Association. If dissatisfied with the Bureau's ruling, the customer could appeal for relief to a full-time Plumbers Licensing Board, composed exclusively of former plumbers now serving in a public capacity. And if dissatisfied with the Board's ruling he could appeal further to a Plumbers Board of Appeals, similarly staffed. It is not difficult to conclude that with such a system in place, tailored to the plumbers' interests, customer dissatisfaction would be endemic. Neither is it difficult to predict that public relations efforts by the Plumbers Trade Association to provide a favorable image for its trade would fall on deaf ears.

To epitomize the heretofore prevailing status of controls over lawyers fees: Clients can't, lawyers won't, courts don't.

8

Lawyers and Their Discontents

Within the past 30 years the legal profession has been hit by two tidal waves, first, the delayed impact of the Industrial Revolution, followed shortly thereafter by the impact of the Information Revolution. The first wave transformed the lawyer-entrepreneur into an organization man, the second the man of learning into an information broker. As the numbers in the profession quadrupled, its prestige ("my son, the lawyer") declined, a decline comparable to that in the status and prestige of the clergy during the nineteenth century.

COLLECTIVIZATION

The changing nature of legal practice has reduced the scope and variety of a lawyer's activities and adversely affected her enjoyment of her work. Today, important legal disputes and transactions are usually addressed through collective efforts of multiple lawyers working as groups rather than as individuals, a result of the concentration of client activities into larger and larger institutions operating under centralized controls. To big business, big government, and big labor have been added mammoth pension funds, mammoth investment funds, mammoth health-care facilities, and mammoth educational institutions. The demands of this mammoth market have changed the face and organization of the legal profession and have changed the available opportunities for individual lawyers to make their way in the profession.

With specialization comes group practice, analogous to the mass production of automobiles, in which under centralized direction groups of workers create and assemble various systems that are then put together to form the finished product. In group legal practice, the role of the individual lawyer lessens. A similar transformation has occurred in other businesses and professions: The former retail store owner is now branch manager in a chain, the former local bank president is now vice president of a multistate financial institution, the once-powerful editor of an independent newspaper has become an employee of a publishing conglomerate, the once-independent doctor increasingly functions as a worker within a group. Such transformation brings with it added constraints on the individual. These include superiors to whom one is answerable, rules that circumscribe independence of action, and collateral powers that must be taken into account (unions, stockholders, environmentalists, minorities). In the history of flight we can see this massive shift in the stature of the once-independent entrepreneur. The Wright brothers conceived, designed, financed, built, tested, and flew the first airplane. A generation later Lindbergh financed, tested, and flew an airplane from New York to Paris. A generation or two later still, men landed on the moon, but their contribution to the flight was limited to piloting a spacecraft under the direction of Mission Control, and their craft was the product of the efforts of thousands of workers paid by the federal government. A comparable transformation has taken place for today's lawyers, who need an organization to function effectively and who, no matter how talented, are usually identified as members of an organization and not as individuals. To an increasing degree a lawyer is viewed as a specialized tool, useful within his particular sphere but not readily employable in others. And with this change in the way lawyers are perceived comes a change in the way they are employed and a rigidity in their available employment. A deputy district attorney prosecuting criminal cases will find limited opportunities for employment in fields other than criminal; a real estate lawyer will find few opportunities outside his specialty. The same is true of the securities specialist, the bankruptcy specialist, and so on. Advertisements offering legal employment tend to be specific. For example, help-wanted ads in the principal Los Angeles legal newspaper announce an intellectual-property firm is seeking a fourth- or fifth-year lawyer with substantial intellectual-property litigation experience; an insurance-coverage litigation firm is seeking a lawyer with two to six years of insurance-coverage litigation experience.[1] Special mention should be made of the plight of the *litigator*, the lawyer in the large law firm who may have spent six to eight years working for her superiors on pleadings, motions, and interrogatories without ever having tried a case. If at the end of that period she is released by the firm, she has few marketable skills and must start her legal career afresh. The plight of the litigator cast adrift is matched by that of the general practitioner, now viewed as a jack-of-all-trades, master of none. To remain functional she, too, must specialize, for her position has become similar to that of the seventeenth-century balladeer, who discovered when fashions changed that poems a-penny-apiece had no market.

DECLINE OF THE LAWYER COUNSELOR

A further change in lawyer status has come about as a result of the lessening use of lawyers as business counselors. As business leaders became better educated and more experienced in affairs outside their own businesses, their reliance on lawyer counselors lessened. The business leader of today may be a graduate of Yale and the Harvard Business School, or may hold a Ph.D. from M.I.T. And through direct experience he may know more about the subtleties of government operations than his lawyer. The business leader himself may be a lawyer who has moved into the business world. Possessing comparable formal education and equally broad experience, he no longer feels the need to rely on a lawyer counselor to reach major decisions. Furthermore, a host of rival counselors now proffer advice to the business-monarch on major decisions, rivals who include corporate general counsel, management consultants, accountants, business economists, financial experts, and legislative experts. Each rival can claim greater expertise in his area than can the lawyer counselor. This conjunction of greater sophistication of business leaders with the rise of specialized consultants covering most major aspects of business decision has produced a sharp decline in the use of lawyers as business advisers and brought about considerable attenuation of the close ties that formerly existed between business leaders and their lawyers. A business leader now employs a variety of consultants for various aspects of a major problem but reserves final decision for himself, or for himself and his principal business associates, in that the erstwhile business monarchy is evolving into cabinet government under which the monarch shares power with an executive committee or an active board of directors. While it remains true that many lawyers continue to serve on corporate boards of directors, their service is becoming increasingly divorced from management and management patronage, in that their obligations to shareholders and others have become increasingly assertive, a development stimulated in part by the growing personal liability of directors for neglect of duty or misconduct. More and more of these lawyer-directors are properly classified as public directors, in that they have no connection with the furnishing of legal services of any sort to the corporations on whose boards they sit. The future role of the lawyer counselor and his firm may be limited to start-up business, where the budding entrepreneur from the workshop, the kitchen, or the garage cannot afford to employ a clutch of consultants. Even here, the lawyer counselor is only one among many possibilities. The accountant may get the job.

DETERIORATION OF LAWYER CANDOR AND CIVILITY

Yet another change in the legal profession is the loss of collegiality among lawyers attendant on the declining effectiveness of informal controls over lawyer conduct. A 1994 RAND survey of California lawyers found that two-thirds of those surveyed believe that lawyers are compromising professionalism and that collegiality and civility among lawyers continue to decline.[2] In an earlier age when communities were smaller and lawyers fewer, lawyers were answerable for their behavior to their colleagues and to the bench, and the law practice of a lawyer who did not keep his word, who lied, who deceived the court, was likely to suffer as news of his delicts became quickly known in the small world in which he moved. The effectiveness of informal controls was directly related to the size of the community—most effective in the smaller towns, least effective in the largest cities. The reason is clear enough. A lawyer distrusted by other lawyers finds it difficult to resolve problems. A lawyer distrusted by judges finds it difficult to get things done in court. In smaller communities, those in which every lawyer is to some extent a personage, distrust of a particular lawyer soon becomes public knowledge, and his practice suffers as clients decide to employ other lawyers who can represent their interests more effectively.

These informal controls still operate in small towns and to a lesser extent in smaller cities. They are also effective in highly-specialized areas of practice in which lawyers do business with the same group of lawyers, clients, and judges, week after week, year after year. In such areas informal controls can remain effective, even in the largest cities. As with traders on a small bourse who deal with one another daily, their word must be as good as their bond. For example, lawyers who practiced admiralty law in San Francisco in the 1950s were a relatively small group, all known to one another. Clients were a concentrated group of shippers, carriers, freight forwarders, and labor representatives, who did business with one another daily. Only seven federal judges had jurisdiction over most admiralty cases. Within this small neighborhood a high degree of trustworthiness, candor, and honesty existed in dealings among its lawyers and with the court, even though the neighborhood was located in the heart of a large metropolis. Each resident of the neighborhood knew that knowledge of any double-dealing or deception in his admiralty practice would rapidly spread to all residents of the neighborhood—lawyers, clients, judges—and that the offending member's practice would suffer as clients reacted to this knowledge by taking their business elsewhere. This general trustworthiness among admiralty lawyers was not based on any superior personal virtue in the lawyers themselves but was the product of repeated dealings with the same set of individuals. A noteworthy feature of these informal controls was that they had no effect outside the practice of admiralty law. The same lawyer who conducted himself honorably in admiralty matters might not hesitate to employ unscrupulous and deceptive means to obtain an immediate advantage in a personal injury or criminal case. This metamorphosis of the Dr. Jekyll in admiralty into the Mr. Hyde in personal injury was directly related to the absence in the latter area of effective informal sanctions for misbehavior.

In today's large cities and metropolitan areas informal controls over lawyer conduct have all but vanished.[3] While in close-knit communities of lawyers and clients there remain pockets of specialized practice where informal sanctions continue to function, these are the exceptions. Los Angeles County and New York City have their tens of thousands of lawyers, most of whom have never seen or heard of one another. In such localities a trial lawyer in general practice may not expect to see the same opposing counsel or the same judge for the next decade. An office lawyer conducting a negotiation may never deal with his counterpart again. A divorce, criminal, or personal injury lawyer may never see his client again. The problems arising from loss of informal controls are compounded by the new mobility of legal practice. A New York lawyer may appear in a Los Angeles court, confident that neither the California courts nor local bar associations can exercise any real control over his conduct and confident that his regulatory counterparts in New York will never become excited over what occurs in California. Under these conditions, candor tends to collapse under the slightest temptation of temporary gain, to the accompaniment of a total loss of civil relations between the lawyers involved. By a kind of Gresham's Law bad manners drive good manners out of circulation, in that the latter involve some inconvenience and exercise of self-control while the former make no such demands. At a minimum, loss of candor and civility in dealings among lawyers makes the profession a less pleasant place to work. But more is involved than loss of the politeness that eases the day's work. Loss of civility connotes loss of respect for one's opponents and for the legal process, and it leads to a loosening of the professional ties that help restrain our more destructive impulses. Such ills are not readily curable by formal sanctions.

OCCUPATIONAL DISCONTENT

These developments in the legal profession, together with the trans-formation that has changed the average lawyer from a known personage in the community to an anonymous man or woman in a gray flannel suit, have produced within the profession a measure of dissatisfaction with law as an occupation. Surveys suggest that half of today's lawyers would enter some other profession or occupation if they could begin again.[4] Some of this sentiment may be the usual grumbling in the ranks, some may come from inflated expectations of the power and earnings of the legal profession, some from long exposure to the drudgery of the law[5] (law students not having been made aware of Lord Brougham's aphorism, "Great lawyer, great drudge"), some from unrealistic expec-tations of the lawyer's influence as reformer and social engineer. In the southern hemisphere of legal practice such discontent is often intensi-fied by the bleakness of the economic landscape. For example, lawyers employed by the Los Angeles district attorney's and public defender's offices in 1996 were considering becoming a local chapter of the United Auto Workers.[6] These surveys probably exaggerate the extent of discon-tent, but there is little reason to doubt that widespread discontent exists, and that two of its causes are the diminished stature of the lawyer in society and the loss of the economic independence formerly attainable by an even moderately successful lawyer.

MONEY AS THE MEASURE OF SUCCESS

These changes have radically reduced the symbols of success in the profession. Public recognition of the lawyer as a person of consequence may never arrive. Status as someone of learning is an artifact of the past. Individual identification apart from law firm affiliation often does not exist. The remaining symbol of success is money. Today, success tends to be judged by income, and the amount of money a lawyer makes becomes the measure of his worth, in his own eyes and in those of his colleagues. The successful law firm specialist, unknown outside a small circle and often anonymous within it, measures his worth by his income and values himself accordingly. The higher he can boost his income, the greater his self-valuation. This might be a harmless vanity, except that each lawyer tends to measure all other lawyers on the same scales. Thus, a two-times-judge's-salary lawyer is nothing special. A four-times-judge's-salary lawyer is an ornament of the bar, and an eight-times-judge's-salary lawyer is a titan of the profession. The heroes of a law firm are the billing partners, those in charge of getting in the money, as differentiated from those who do the actual work. Such legal glorifica-tion of billing partners contrasts sharply with that in engineering firms, whose heroes are the project engineers, those in charge of getting the work done.

This preoccupation with money as the sole measure of success, with its spectacle of lawyers driven by dollars, provides a precarious foundation for a lawyer's self-respect and self-confidence. And the quest for money, when fueled by insecurity, has its ugly side, which may surface not only in abusive dealings with clients and opposing lawyers, as mentioned earlier, but also in dealings with fellow lawyers within the same firm. Abusive dealings within a law firm over money and billing credits may disrupt the quality and integrity of its operations and even jeopardize the firm's continued existence. On a primitive level mistrust among members of a law firm has produced such comic situations as the three-partner San Francisco criminal defense law firm that had three office safes, one in each partner's room. On a more sophisticated level it can result in alteration or suppression of a law firm's internal records, false reports of oral dealings within the firm, and covert or overt accusations of dishonesty directed against other lawyers in the firm.

Two explanations for these several abuses are current. The first is that today's lawyers, in contrast to those of yesteryear, are greedy for money and do not hesitate to stoke their cupidity; the second is that those earlier leaders of the bar who acted as beau ideals for their contemporaries to emulate, who were willing to sacrifice their own immediate interests for the general public good, have disappeared and have not been replaced. Both explanations preach slightly different texts of the same gospel. Put together, they combine a moral vision of lawyers as fallen angels profaned by avarice and greed with a romantic vision of lawyers redeemed by future saints within their ranks, capable as in the past of heroic self-denial in the service of the public good.

Here we find the perennial myth of Hesiod's Golden Age, always located in the past, always superior to our own Iron Age. It is a theme argued by John Milton in *Paradise Lost* (how fallen, how changed from . . . transcendent brightness) and by Edmund Burke in *Reflections on the Revolution in France* (The age of chivalry is gone, and that of sophisters, economists, and calculators has succeeded).[7] Cicero's lament in a corrupt age for the great days of the Republic (*O tempora, o mores*), and Chief Justice Crewe's lament in troubled Stuart times for the disappearance of a strong feudal nobility (Where is Mowbray, where is Mortimer, where is the great Plantagenet?)[8] find echoes in the current mournful dirge bewailing the disappearance of the lawyer-statesman, the public-spirited counselor ever-mindful of the larger interests of the community.

Some years ago Thurman W. Arnold in his classroom pointed out the irresistible attraction of the immediate or not too distant past, whose merits are extolled, whose defects are forgotten. The attitude is part nostalgia, buttressed by a comparison of the best of the past with the average of the present (a comparison in which, not surprisingly, the present always runs a distant second), and part reluctance to accept the prosaic compromises that have always constituted part of daily life. Such comparisons of taught ideal with experienced reality leads to the easy conclusion that (statesmanship) (business morals) (integrity) (professionalism) have been sliding downhill, a conclusion apt to be reached by each new generation. "Where is Churchill, where is de Gaulle, where is the great Roosevelt?" is the plaint in political spheres, echoed in legal circles by "Where is Henry L. Stimson, John W. Davis, the great Charles Evans Hughes?"

A heavenly glow envelops our favorite legal Golden Age, and we forget the failings of earlier times. Forgotten is the undercurrent of violence that accompanied American legal practice in the first half of the nineteenth century, even among its best lawyers—Aaron Burr, Andrew Jackson, Stephen Field, David S. Terry, the last of whom as Chief Justice of the California Supreme Court always displayed a loaded revolver on the bench while holding court.[9] Forgotten is the judicial, legislative, and witness chicanery that tainted much of the activity of railroad, mining, and patent lawyers in the second half of the nineteenth century. And forgotten is the elementary fact that since the beginnings of the legal profession the first aim of practicing law has been to make enough money to earn a living. That the characters of contemporary lawyers are any worse than those of prior generations is a dubious proposition. The legal profession contains a few heroes, a few scoundrels, and every gradation between. Over the years the proportions of good and bad have not changed. Lawyer-statesmen such as Cyrus Vance, Warren Christopher, and Lloyd Cutler grace public life today as capably as did Thomas E. Dewey, Dean Acheson, and John J. McCloy a generation earlier, and as did Louis D. Brandeis, George Wharton Pepper, and George W. Wickersham a generation before that.

The vision of a Golden Age of legal practice ill serves the interests of lawyers and clients alike, in that under the spell of this vision proposals to restore harmonious conditions in the practice of law are apt to lack realism and rely instead on effecting changes in human nature. It does little good to fulminate against the declining character of the current generation of lawyers, to decry loss of civic virtue and social responsibility, and to propose quixotic enterprises to recreate an idealized law practice of the past. What has changed in the legal profession are the terms, conditions and circumstances under which lawyers function. What needs to be done to restore values, harmony, and satisfaction within the profession is to adapt the operations, expectations, and rewards of the profession to its new surroundings.

9

The Pervasive Public Distrust of Lawyers

Why is there always a secret singing
When a lawyer cashes in?
Why does a hearse horse snicker
Hauling a lawyer away?

Carl Sandburg[1]

From the time lawyers first organized into guilds and secured a monopoly over delivery of legal services, they have been objects of suspicion and targets of unflattering comment by a sizable portion of the population. In part this distaste is an inevitable byproduct of the lawyer's principal function, to champion one party to a controversy and enable him to prevail over his opponent. By a process of transference the divorcing husband may grow to hate his wife's lawyer more than the wife, the suing businessman the competitor's lawyer more than the competitor, the heir the contesting relative's lawyer more than the relative, and the public the defense lawyer more than the accused. In these and similar instances of controversy the lawyer is either perceived as the wrongdoer himself or one seeking to shield the wrongdoer from just retribution. Thus at any given time a segment of the population will be irate at particular lawyers and, by an easy extension, irate at all lawyers. Nothing new here: It is the familiar story of hostility against the messenger who delivers the bad news. Formerly, this anger against an opposing lawyer was offset to some degree by admiration and respect for the party's own lawyer, often viewed as a guard dog vigilantly resisting the ravages of the lawyer-wolves who prowled the forest. On balance, most of the population classified lawyers as necessary evils, like taxes and parking meters, no better no worse than the general run of mankind. But today there exists a pervasive distrust of all lawyers, a distrust that now includes one's own lawyer, a distrust that manifests itself in the growing number of legal malpractice suits filed by clients against their own lawyers. Survey after survey reflects this distrust. For example, a 1995 *U.S. News & World Report* survey reported that 69 percent of its sampling said "lawyers are only sometimes honest or not usually honest."[2] Much of the general public sees lawyers as possessing the morals of a campaign consultant and the manners of an investigative reporter.

In at least one earlier time public distrust of lawyers had become similarly widespread. With the decline of feudalism in England in the fifteenth century and the accompanying collapse of effective government, manipulation of the legal system by lawyers and use of pressure tactics by litigants became common occurrences. The period was, says William Holdsworth, a savagely litigious age in which legal chicanery and trumped-up charges became regular weapons of offense and defense.[3] Such tactics are known as champerty (stirring up and creating litigation) and maintenance (supporting, promoting, and financing litigation). As a consequence of widespread use of such tactics the law came to be viewed as oppressive and lawyers seen as instruments and beneficiaries of that oppression. Shakespeare's depiction of Jack Cade's agenda ("the first thing we do, let's kill all the lawyers") is a dramatization of popular feeling expressed in Cade's own proclamation of 1450 ("The law serves nothing else in these days but to do wrong, for almost nothing progresses except false matters by mede [bribe], drede [fear] and favor").[4] On reestablishment of stable government by the Tudors one of their first acts in 1487 was to improve the legal system by a strengthened enforcement of the criminal laws against champerty and maintenance.[5]

There are parallels with events of today. During the past 100 years the laws against champerty and maintenance have become so weakened that these activities, once criminal, are now deemed no more than indiscretions, worthy of reproof only when carried to an extreme of bad taste. Champerty and maintenance, also known as barratry and embracery, tend to overlap, but the core distinction appears to be between champerty as activity within the legal system (solicitation, initiation, and manipulation of lawsuits) and maintenance as activity outside the legal system (steps to exert pressure on the legal system to influence its re-

sults). Today, even though the mechanics of champerty and maintenance have greatly changed from those used in medieval England, both
are alive and in good health. Champerty takes the form of solicitation
of relatives at the sites of airplane crashes and other disasters, of lawyer
advertisements for clients with grievances against specific employers,
institutions, and commercial products, of initiation and financing of
speculative lawsuits in the hope wrongdoing will turn up. Not only are
all expenses for certain kinds of litigation carried by lawyers with no
client obligation to pay except from the proceeds of a successful outcome, but in many class actions, derivative actions, and pro bono litigation, the lawyers themselves are the only real beneficiaries of success.
Maintenance today seldom relies on armed followers and threats of violence against witnesses, jurors, or judges to influence the outcome of
a suit, but uses outside events to influence what happens inside the
courtroom—demonstrations, pickets, protest meetings, press conferences, news leaks, lawyer media appearances, talk-show participations,
favors for the press, and staged dramatic events for television. The spin,
originally an election tactic to influence voters, has become a legal tactic
to influence judges and jurors. Bar associations and law groups now
conduct lawyer seminars and prepare videotapes on methods of influ-
encing and using the news media.[6] Over time the public has become
well aware of these activities, and its respect for the legal profession has
plummeted, a view shared by lawyers themselves. The 1994 RAND survey reported that over half of California's lawyers believe that advertising
has contributed to the decline of professionalism.[7] A representative sign
of this change is the reluctance of California legislators to list themselves
as lawyers, an identification that has shifted from an asset to a liability
in electoral politics.[8]

Corporate clients of law firms share this pervasive distrust of lawyers.
In business circles distrust of lawyers, especially lawyer-promoters of
class-action and mass-tort lawsuits, has approached the level of distrust
of professional informers (*delatores*) in ancient Rome, who were seen as
initiators of litigation designed to produce profit through denunciation,
who were described by Gibbon as legal assassins.[9] A 1986 American Bar
Association survey found that only 6 percent of corporations rated all
or most lawyers as deserving of being called professionals.[10] For example, David Pace Jr. of Affiliated Computer Services, citing instances of
overstaffing and overcompartmentalization, concluded that large law
firms have "an institutional disregard for cost," distort fees through leverage, and may churn cases with unnecessary tasks. Peter Zeughauser
of the Irvine Company commented that some lawyers, good lawyers
whose work he respects, are fee abusers, and he asserted that "fee abuse
is an incurable disease." The solution both men propose is "litigation

management," a careful monitoring of the work of their own lawyers to identify and prevent abuses.[11]

The primary cause of this distrust of lawyers is money. The pervasive lack of candor over fees and charges in matters great and small sows the dragon's teeth of distrust between lawyers and clients, who now feel they must keep one eye on their opponent's lawyer and the other on their own, that both need watching. We have seen the virtually unlimited possibilities of abuse attached to hourly billings. Although a client cannot tell how much time a lawyer actually spends preparing a given pleading, he does know of discrepancies between events in which he personally participated and those same events as depicted in hourly billings. A three-minute phone call may be charged as one of 12, 18, or 24 minutes. An hour's conference may be charged as three hours. In a conference between two of his lawyers one may report a two-hour billing, the other four hours.[12]

Distrust arises when a client who has agreed to pay rates of $150 to $500 an hour for his lawyer's services discovers that he is also expected to pay substantial items of the lawyer's overhead and that he had not understood the true cost of the engagement. Moreover, the calculation of chargeable lawyer hours may not have been made clear. The lawyer who travels from his base in Washington to San Francisco on behalf of a client may bill from the time of leaving Dulles International Airport to the time of return, thereby producing 24-hour, sometimes 27-hour, days. The vice here is inadequate advance disclosure. Had the lawyer in the beginning fully identified the true costs the client would incur during the course of the engagement, he could have avoided misunderstandings. On the other hand, full disclosure of true costs in advance might convince the client to go elsewhere. Too often the path adopted is to get the client inside the door with what appears an acceptable fee, and only later, after the client has committed himself to the services, to disclose the true costs. When eventually the client learns what the total costs are, he often feels he has been the victim of a sophisticated version of bait-and-switch or, to put it more delicately, that the lawyer had been less than economically responsible in his disclosure of the probable cost of the services. And if the client further discovers that some of these costs represent a theoretical law firm outlay (such as rent of the law firm's own conference room) or are disbursements to which an undisclosed profit markup has been added, he may conclude he has been defrauded.

Client distrust can also arise upon discovery of different charges to different clients for identical services. As noted earlier, a lawyer's hourly rate is self-declared and not graven in stone. A knowledgeable client through bazaar haggling may secure a lower rate from the law firm before committing for the services. An unsophisticated client may take the lawyer's evaluation of his services at face value and agree to pay it. If that client later discovers that other clients are being charged less for the same services, his confidence in the candor and integrity of the lawyer and the law firm he has employed will be shaken. Client distrust may also arise when a law firm engages in sharp practice on behalf of its own client. The client will accept the benefit of any resulting gain but at the same time remain uneasy that at some future time sharp practice may be employed against him. For example, in contract disputes where the contract has specified that the loser will pay the winner's legal fees, a law firm may represent a client under a tacit agreement that the client will pay modest fees but that huge fees will be regularly billed to the client, payable only if the client wins and the court awards them as costs to the prevailing party. In effect, the parties have colluded to saddle excessive fees on the opposing litigant in the event of victory. While such collusion serves the client's immediate interests, it does nothing to fortify his trust in the integrity of the law firm that structured such an arrangement. A comparable distrust and resentment arises among real estate borrowers when lawyers selected by real estate lenders (banks, etc.) charge premium fees to the borrowers for routine services, fees the borrowers must pay if they are to get their loans.[13]

A chronic source of lawyer distrust arises in contingent-fee actions in which the lawyer's fee is set as a percentage of the recovery, most often 33 percent. Most clients understand recovery to mean net recovery, after costs and expenses have been satisfied. A rude awakening may come when the successful client discovers that the lawyer's percentage applies to gross and not net recovery. Thus in a $100,000 judgment where costs and expenses have been $50,000, the lawyer's fee will be $33,000 and the client's share $17,000 instead of the other way around as the client expected. At the moment of recovery a contingent-fee client is usually glad to get anything; only later does the client conclude he has been diddled. In California, although not in all states, the legislature has made this particular scam more difficult by requiring that all fee contracts be in writing, that the client be told the percentage for the lawyer's fee is open to bargaining, and that the method of accounting for costs and expenses be made clear.[14]

Contingent-fee contracts give lawyers a direct interest in the proceeds of any recovery, and when multiple lawyers represent the same claimant, as often happens in large claims, a successful claimant's receipt of money may be substantially delayed by disputes among her own lawyers over the division of legal fees.[15] And in class actions the costs in multi-claimant suits may be charged against the first claimant to recover, as in a breast-implant case where of $6 million paid to settle one claim against Dow Corning before its bankruptcy the claimant received only $1.8 million.[16]

Contingent-fee scams are the occupational weakness of solo lawyers and small law firms practicing in the southern legal hemisphere. Creative accounting and misleading billings are the occupational weakness of large law firms in the northern hemisphere. Such prestigious firms as Cravath Swaine (New York), Skadden Arps (New York), Weil Gotshal (New York), Latham & Watkins (Los Angeles), Sidley & Austin (Chicago), Winston & Strawn (Chicago), and Mayer Brown (Chicago) have had their reputations tarnished by instances of overcharges and excessive fee demands, publicly identified as such in formal proceedings.[17] Other law firms, for example, Gibson Dunn (Los Angeles), have become involved in protracted litigation with former clients who claim to have been victimized by overcharges.[18] The foregoing roster includes six of the country's ten largest law firms in 1994.[19] The former managing partner of Winston & Strawn pleaded guilty to felony charges connected with fees, as did the former managing partner of Rose Law Firm, the then largest law firm in Little Rock, who earlier in his career had served as chairman of the ethics committee of the Arkansas Bar Association.[20] The legal columns of *The Wall Street Journal, The New York Times, The Washington Post*, and the national and local legal press periodically report such transgressions as they become matters of public record. It has been observed there is no great difference between overbilling a client and misappropriating a client's money.[21] In defense of these firms it must be noted that increases in the size of a law firm increase the possibilities of improper conduct within the firm, including representation of conflicting interests when one of its lawyers has been unwilling to forgo a fee. Activities of lawyers in the hundreds and of support staff in greater numbers are difficult to supervise, and just as misconduct regularly occurs among the 535 members of Congress and has occurred in the federal judiciary and in the highest state courts of Pennsylvania, Illinois, Texas, Rhode Island, New York, and Oklahoma, so some misconduct is inevitable in any large organization. The foregoing explains but does not excuse the frequency of such incidents in large law firms. The analogy between public-office misbehavior and lawyer misbehavior in law firms is misleading. Congress and the courts are not organized as voluntary associations whose members come together to perform their work. Rather they are bodies selected by outsiders (voters, governors, presidents), whose members can be removed only through heroic effort. By contrast, a law firm as a private association can sever its relationship with a particular lawyer at the first hint of impropriety. A well-run law firm's record for integrity should greatly surpass that of any public body.

The public perception of lawyer overreaching is heightened by applications for fees by individual lawyers and small law firms in highly-publicized civil rights cases, fee applications that possess little of the verisimilitude of the computer runs used by large law firms and that ask for the sun, moon, and stars. Because these applications usually seek to draw on public funds they are not kindly received by the public or by the courts. For example, in Rodney King's application for lawyers' fees against the City of Los Angeles for the services of the twenty-four lawyers and four paralegals who worked on his civil case, the $4.4 million sought was reduced to $1.6 million, his two principal lawyers each being awarded a fifth of the amounts they asked for.[22] The principal lasting effect of such fee applications is to fortify the negative public perception of all lawyers.

The foregoing strongly suggests that fee charges are the principal cause of public distrust of lawyers and will remain so until the present practices and incentives that foster excessive charges change. Sol Linowitz, emphasizing the decline of a lawyer professionalism that now uncritically accepts client objectives at face value and allows the ethics of the criminal bar to dominate large law firm litigation, has similarly concluded that money is at the heart of the legal profession's problems.[23] To put it bluntly, until the present laissez-faire attitude of the bar toward picking a client's pockets through overcharges is superseded by the more realistic view that overcharging is first cousin to theft, public distrust of lawyers will remain at its present barometric low.

What of the future?

10

Through a Glass Darkly

During the past thirty years we have experienced an uncontrolled and largely unplanned growth in law firm size among providers of mainstream legal services. This growth was accompanied by commercialization of law practice, relaxation of traditional professional restraints, and obsession with money as the measure of professional success. We have seen mainstream fees and practices set the pace for legal fees of every description. But this brave new world of the large privately-owned law firm has been plagued by firm instability, by increased lawyer dissatisfaction within its ranks, by growing public distrust of all lawyers, and by general client dissatisfaction with escalating costs of legal services. The principal causes of increased legal costs have been client and public inertia and lack of incentive within the legal world to upset a state of affairs under which lawyers have prospered. Change must originate outside the legal system and be driven by forces that are strongly motivated to effect it. Its twin movers must be the clients who pay the bills and the public that bears the costs. On effective mobilization of these outside forces, four future developments affecting the cost and means of delivery of legal services are probable.

Clients will balk at excessive fees and pay premium fees only for premium services. Because today's clients are rapidly acquiring the skills to protect their own interests, premium fees, set by lawyers and accepted by courts, will cease to be the norm.

Clients will press public executives and legislatures for legal reform. These bodies in turn will press courts to take a more active role in making legal procedures less dilatory and less costly.

In response to client and court demands for services that are cost-effective, competition among large law firms and other providers of legal services will further intensify.

Individual lawyers will seek out legal workplaces that provide opportunities for full professional development and offer the most satisfactory and enjoyable way of practicing law.

We have seen the large privately-owned law firm develop into the ringmaster of the profession. For that reason our analysis of the legal profession's future will focus primarily on the large law firm's future, to which the remainder of the profession is now adjunct. Will large privately-owned law firms continue to dominate the center ring, or are their weaknesses such that they will be exiled from the big tent to sideshow status? The answer depends on how effectively these firms respond to the four major challenges they now face.

11

First Challenge: Client Control of Fees

In any consensual system for exchange of goods or services, if the buyer is willing to pay without objection the amount the seller asks, that amount becomes the contract price, and if absence of bargaining over price is general, that price becomes the norm. But if a buyer rejects the asking price as unacceptable and succeeds in getting it reduced, either by dealing with the initial seller or one of his competitors, and if other buyers are similarly successful, the new lower price becomes the norm. So it is with legal services. In arranging for legal services clients in the past have not been strongly motivated to conduct serious bargaining, and even when so inclined have been handicapped by their lack of legal sophistication. Much of the responsibility for the accelerated rise in legal fees during the past 30 years may be placed on the doorstep of the indifferent corporate client. But recent seedlings of change display rapid and vigorous growth of client desires and capabilities to bring about a new relationship.

CLIENT INCENTIVE

Client motivation to control legal costs has been powerfully stimulated by the increased proportion that legal costs now bear of the total cost of doing business. The impact of this increased share has been intensified by the now-familiar presence of bet-the-store litigation. Product liability, as with medical devices (E. H. Robins), cosmetic devices (Dow Corning), asbestos injuries (Johns Manville), environmental pollution, as with major oil spills, and disputes over the purchase and sale of giant businesses (Texaco) can send major corporations into bankruptcy. Hostile takeovers, unsought mergers, maneuvers threatening corporate extinction, and claims of major fraud in securities flotation or financial reporting can lead to huge legal expenditures. The cost of prosecuting or defending these claims may be of such magnitude that no properly-run corporation can avoid giving them close scrutiny. For example, in 1993 Bristol-Myers Squibb Company recorded a special charge of $1.5 billion for liabilities and expenses related to the defense of breast-implant claims, offset by $1 billion of expected insurance proceeds.[1]

At the same time that costs of legal services have been increasing as a proportion of total costs of doing business, the luster of large law firms has been dimmed by a series of episodes that reflect adversely on the competence or integrity of some of these firms. These serve as a continuing reminder to clients that large law firms, like other large organizations, can make mistakes, do mediocre work, and harbor individual lawyers who must be watched. Such episodes dissipate some of the mystique that formerly attached to these firms and stimulate clients to examine law firm performance and legal costs the same way they examine performance and cost of other vendors and suppliers.

CLIENT ABILITIES

Accompanying this increased client motivation for control of legal costs is increased client ability to evaluate the worth of legal services, both in quality and in cost. At the forefront of this ability is the spectacular rise in the legal and business world of the status and quality of corporate general counsel. In earlier generations, lawyers employed full time in corporate law departments were, like ships' doctors, generally seen as second tier, a view that took on the dimensions of a self-fulfilling prophecy, one epitomized by a motion-picture mogul's evaluation of his house counsel in the 1930s: "If they were any good, they wouldn't be working for me." Since then a sea change has occurred, and, much as the barber-surgeon rose from humble station to rank equally with the doctor of physic, so corporate counsel now rank on a par with private counsel. This ranking is reflected in the fact that the median compensation of chief legal officers in corporate law departments now exceeds the median of senior lawyers in private practice.[2] The current corporate practice of paying its general counsel the same compensation he or she could earn in private practice, plus generous retirement benefits, stock options, and other perks not available in private law firms, has enabled large corporations such as General Electric and IBM to attract top-flight senior lawyers from private law firms, not only as general counsel but as chiefs of various legal specialties within their law departments. General counsel are beginning to appear more frequently as members of the board of directors of the corporation they serve. Direct consultation between outside directors and the corporation's general counsel periodically takes place. Corporate counsel, with legal knowledge, experience, prestige, and skills equal to the most senior members of large law firms, are able to bargain on even terms with the law firms that handle major segments of the corporation's legal business. Such bargaining is occurring more frequently and vigorously than in the past, as corporate general counsel, under pressure from their superiors to reduce costs, act to earn their keep.[3]

Where large corporations blaze the trail, middle-sized corporations follow. In the bargaining over costs of legal services we can expect a return to the normal competitive state of business dealings, under which a purchaser with several vendors to choose from possesses an equal voice over price. This development does not imply that corporate counsel will supersede outside counsel; it merely indicates a rival force has been gathering strength in the business world that operates as a check and balance on the formerly unchallenged position of outside counsel. The combination of increased client incentive and increased client ability to control legal costs is beginning to have a powerful impact on the price of legal services, on premium and excessive legal fees, and on the size and composition of corporate law departments, many of which now have staffs of hundreds of lawyers.[4]

Corporate counsel are now experimenting with a variety of tools to monitor and control legal activities to make them cost-effective.[5] These tools include increased in-house staff, temporary in-house employment of lawyers, computer audits of lawyers' bills, allocation of comparable legal work among different law firms and in-house counsel to compare costs, competitive bidding among law firms, and use of fixed-fee contracts for specific legal services (a partial return to nineteenth-century practices). A growing custom is to divide legal work in a particular case between house counsel and outside counsel on the basis of what each does best. For example, General Motors' law department prepares briefs and argument covering issues of product liability for adaptation by trial counsel in pending cases throughout the country. The result is high-quality argument on product liability in each case, and a saving in legal costs to General Motors through elimination of duplicate research on the same general issues.

Some clients continue to accept billable hours as the basis for fees but impose specific limits on what they will recognize as billable hours. Some will not pay for a lawyer's services in excess of 10 hours a day; some insist only one lawyer appear at depositions; some that only specified lawyers work on their business; some require advance authorization for particular expenses, such as out-of-town trips; some demand the most favorable rate the law firm charges any other client. Clients who continue to accept billable hours may refuse to pay for lawyer travel-time and may reject extra charges for secretarial overtime, automated legal research, and the like as services already included within the hourly rates.[6] Some clients will not pay for the services of first- or second-year lawyers, arguing that the law firm should train beginning lawyers at its own expense. As clients become more knowledgeable, they become more discriminating in their selection of lawyers within a firm to work on their projects, and increasingly they exercise this discrimination. Like a rich man who gets his suits from Savile Row and neckties from Sulka but buys sports clothes from Levi Strauss and underwear from Sears, a client may employ premium-priced lawyers and law firms for extraordinary services and competitively-priced lawyers and law firms for routine services. This practice, known as cherry picking, is a subject of much grousing among law firms but one that forcefully draws their attention to the need for periodic fee adjustments to keep their firms and their lawyers price-competitive.

Client evaluation and client control of fees present a direct threat to the large law firm's current practice of leverage, under which law firm costs for the services of its juniors may be marked up 100 percent or more. Since at any given time prevailing rates of pay for younger lawyers in a given locality are generally known to knowledgeable house counsel, as are costs of law office overhead, it is no great problem for a client to calculate law firm production costs for the services of specific lawyers and in effect bargain over the amount of the markup. Some clients have even sued to challenge the amount of these markups as unconscionable, suits defended by law firms as involving matters that are none of the clients' business.[7] Regardless of the outcomes of such suits, sophisticated clients will undoubtedly continue to bargain aggressively in the area of markups.

A few specific examples illustrate the changing lawyer-client relationship resulting from client efforts to reduce legal costs.

- Sally F. King, legal administrator of General Electric, acting under company pressure to cut costs of outside legal fees, describes the adoption by GE of a system of fee discounts and bonuses tied to the efficiency of a law firm's work, of reliance on specific lawyers of known capability within a law firm rather than on the firm itself, of refusal to pay for services of first- or second-year lawyers ("They can put them on our matters, we just don't want to pay for them''), of joint case management between GE and outside counsel (number of depositions, etc.), and of greater use of direct electronic communications to reduce travel costs. The company is also considering movement away from fees based on hourly billings. But, she reports, GE disagrees with the notion of legal auditing in that auditing puts lawyer and client in an adversarial relationship. She sees the remedy for fee abuses as a switch in law firms.[8]

- Zoë Baird, general counsel of Aetna Life, sees the growing climate of distrust between lawyer and client as arising from the growing divergence between charges for legal services and their value to the client—the result, she believes, of the perverse incentives of hourly billing. Aetna no longer accepts hourly billing as the predominant method of pricing legal services, believing that hours spent are no measure of productivity, that results are a better measure. Her substitute is value billing, which includes early budgets, fixed-fee arrangements for different segments of litigation, incentive bonuses, and modified contingency arrangements, all in an attempt to link pay to performance.[9]

- Peter Kujawski, counsel for Travelers Group (stockbrokerage, financial services, insurance), describes his company's cost-cutting measures in the procurement of outside legal services. These include task-based billing, use of no more than one senior and one junior lawyer on any given matter (unless otherwise agreed), use of a single lawyer at depositions, the benefit of the most favorable rate the firm charges any other client, and employment of legal auditors to monitor charges. Such prestigious New York firms as Simpson Thacher and Skadden Arps, he reports, have agreed to follow Travelers' new policy.[10]

- Brokerage of competitive bidding may be in the offing. Lexis Counsel Connect advertises an e-mail service at no cost to the client to ''let a short list of experienced lawyers bid on your next engagement'' and describes its service as a new marketplace ''based on quality and value, not simply old-boy connections and hourly time charges.''[11]

Additionally, legislatures are beginning to make available to clients, large and small, opportunities to exercise greater control over legal fees than has been practicable heretofore. California has created a nonbinding arbitration system for disputed legal fees, the use of which is compulsory for lawyers but voluntary for clients.[12] Although the system is administered by bar associations, its rules first authorized and now require every three-member arbitration panel to include one lay member. Moreover, pilot projects are experimenting with use of panels of two lay members and one lawyer. Use of this system of arbitration is giving clients an increasingly effective voice over fees. Is a fee too high? Don't pay it and demand arbitration.

As yet there can be no assurance that these remedies will deliver the cost-effectiveness their backers anticipate, in that many are largely mechanical and deal only with the surface aspect of excessive fees. Quality and thoroughness of performance may be skimped; fees may be lightly front-loaded and heavily back-loaded; trust and confidence between house counsel and outside counsel may be difficult to maintain. Much experimentation will be needed to find out which of these remedies works in fact. It may be that client control of fees will prove effective for routine work, less so for skilled, imaginative work.

While it cannot be said with certainty that any single one of these remedies leads to cost-effectiveness, there are indications that as a group they are taking hold. Increases in large-corporation legal spending reportedly leveled off in 1994 to well below the rate of inflation.[13] More and more clients are insisting on replacement of the iron gauntlet of billable hours with a flexible work glove capable of providing a better cost-benefit ratio for legal expenses. These experiments are generating strong pressure on lawyers to make their operations more cost-effective.

12

Second Challenge: Increased Court Control over Legal Proceedings and Lawyer Conduct

Pressures on law firms to lower costs of legal services are also coming from the courts, which in turn are responding to pressures from legislative and administrative bodies and to growing threats to the courts' own monopoly of adjudication. These dual forces are impelling courts to play an increasingly active role in containing the escalating costs of legal proceedings.

DIRECT PRESSURES ON COURTS TO REDUCE LEGAL COSTS

In past years the principal pressures on courts relating to legal services have come from trial lawyers and lawyer-dominated legislatures, and the thrust of these pressures has been on the side of exhaustive legal proceedings and handsome remuneration for legal services, with only passing attention given to the usefulness and cost-effectiveness of the proceedings themselves. These past legislative pressures on courts generally focused on the interests of producers of legal services (lawyers) and not on those of consumers of legal services (clients), in large part because lawyer organizations were the only groups active in this area. Sporadic moves for legal reform, lacking support from powerful pressure groups, usually resulted in a slow waltz of one step forward, two steps backward. For example, in 1975 a Los Angeles group seeking to reduce the length and cost of civil jury trials in California courts proposed legislation to reduce the number of peremptory challenges to jurors from six to three, the latter being the allowable number in federal courts. But active support for this change did not extend beyond academic and good-government circles, and the proposed change ran contrary to the views of the strong trial-lawyer lobby, which reflected the perceived interest of trial lawyers in controlling jury proceedings and ensuring comprehensive, even exhaustive, trials. New legislation on the subject was ultimately adopted, but rather than reducing peremptory challenges, their number was increased from six to eight.[1] So much for legislative reform unsupported by effective pressure groups.

Today, however, pressures on legislatures to reduce waste, duplication, and delay in the courts are coming from powerful groups that perceive their interests to be adversely affected by current practices. These groups include retailers, manufacturers, professionals rendering services, and consumers, each operating through associations and employing professional lobbyists. Inclusion of consumers in the list might be thought erroneous, in that past activities by highly-publicized groups of lawyers purporting to speak for consumers have given the impression that consumers are opposed to any reduction in the cost and expense of litigation that might jeopardize Melvin Belli's "more adequate award."[2] This view of consumer alignment is so widespread that in 1995 the California Trial Lawyers Association, a lobbying group for trial-lawyer interests, recognizing the disrepute into which trial lawyers had fallen, changed its name to the Consumer Attorneys of California in order to be identified with the interests of consumers and not those of lawyers. In point of fact, consumer interests are ambivalent, in that as buyers of goods and services they must pay prices that reflect the costs of providing those goods and services. For example: operators of ski lifts have been subject to frequent suits for personal injuries by those injured while skiing, who plead failure to warn of the hazards of the sport, the terrain, and so on, with the result that the cost of lift tickets escalated beyond the means of many skiers. Thereafter, as a consequence of pressures from ski-lift operators and skiing groups alike, Colorado and Utah adopted ski-at-your-own-risk laws in an attempt to keep the cost of lift tickets within affordable bounds, the Colorado legislature declaring that skiing contributes to the economy of the state and that claims, litigation, and threats thereof unnecessarily increase costs.[3] The same factors writ large appear in the area of health care, where consumers of health care are active on all fronts, including the legal front, to reduce costs.

Additional pressures on courts to become more efficient arise from government budgetary constraints. In past years whenever complaints about the law's delays and expense reached respectable decibels, legislatures responded by creating more courts and more judges, thereby allowing the luxury of wasteful and expensive litigation practices to continue. With today's pressures on all government budgets, legislatures have embraced the idea of more efficient and less wasteful use of existing facilities, and through new legislation and stricter rules of procedure they are putting direct pressure on the courts to reform court practices and become more cost-effective. Just as in the Roman Empire the pressure of invading Huns on the territories of the Goths resulted in pressure by the Goths on the Roman frontiers, so the pressures of clients and budgets on legislatures result in turn in legislative pressures on courts to make legal processes cost-effective. To preserve their adjudication empires, courts are being forced to respond.

INDIRECT PRESSURES ON COURTS FROM RIVAL TRIBUNALS

A second source of pressure on courts to achieve cost-effectiveness comes from the growing competition of rival adjudication systems, which include other courts and tribunals and private methods of dispute resolution. Here an element of self-preservation comes into play.

For the first hundred years of our nation, the country's legal system operated with what amounted to one set of courts of general jurisdiction, the state courts, supplemented by federal courts with limited jurisdiction over such specialized areas of law as admiralty, patents, customs, and federal law. But with the growing centralization of the country during the second hundred years and the growing reach of the federal government, the once-limited sphere of the federal courts steadily expanded, with the result that direct competition arose between state and federal court systems. In this competition federal courts have had most of the advantages. Their judges are usually better paid and more rigorously selected, possess superior support staff and courthouse facilities, and by reason of life tenure are less susceptible to external pressures. In most regions of the country federal courts are perceived as better courts than their state counterparts, and as a consequence of this perception they draw important legal business away from state courts of general jurisdiction. This perception extends to Congress itself, which since the days of Reconstruction has given the federal courts jurisdiction over new legislation of national importance to ensure the new law's effective enforcement. Recent examples include assassination of federal officers,[4] racketeering,[5] and terrorism.[6]

Competition with courts of general jurisdiction also comes from the adjudicating activities of administrative tribunals and specialized courts. Such bodies come into existence when courts are seen as doing an unsatisfactory job in a particular area in terms of promptness, cost, and reliability of decision. The consequence has been removal, in whole or in part, of large areas of decision making from the courts to other tribunals. Workers' compensation and unpaid wage claims are past examples. A potential future loss of court business is automobile accident compensation, a category that comprises a major share of civil cases filed in state courts. Most independent observers agree that the existing system of compensation produces results that are unpredictable, uneconomical, and wasteful. It continues in its current form only because there is no consensus yet on a replacement.

In recent years private methods of resolving disputes have also flourished. These, too, provide increased competition for existing court systems. The oldest and best-known of these methods is binding arbitration, whose virtues include prompt adjudication and low cost. Other methods of private adjudication cover a range of devices generally described as alternative dispute resolution, which are variations of mediation in which disputants employ an impartial third party to promote and bring about a voluntary settlement of their dispute. The mechanics of this exercise in persuasion may include an abbreviated mock trial designed to expose a client to the potential weakness of his own position and the potential strength of the opposing side. A recent hybrid of public and private adjudication is agreement of the parties to employ a retired judge to try their pending dispute under court rules and render an enforceable judgment. This procedure, known as "rent-a-judge," gives litigants a speedy trial before a judge of their own choosing and, until recent years, an ability to try their case in private, the latter a feature of great attraction to Hollywood celebrities involved in domestic disputes.[7] However, changes in California statutes and court rules have made public access to such proceedings mandatory. Numerous private organizations have come into being to organize and operate these competing systems, among them JAMS/Endispute, a profit corporation owned by the venture capital firm of Warburg, Pincus & Co.[8]

This two-front challenge to courts of general jurisdiction presents competition of such magnitude that in time it could reduce the business of state courts to a potpourri of local events, local crime, domestic relations, and decedents' estates. Neither can state courts take survival itself for granted, in that a federal system of government need not necessarily maintain two sets of overlapping court systems, as the Canadian and Australian federal systems of a single set of courts illustrate. These gloomy possibilities have largely arisen from past failures of state courts to simplify and modernize their ways of conducting business to prevent process from overshadowing substance. Yet these courts possess powerful competitive advantages of their own. Unlike arbitrators and professional mediators, their judges do not possess private ties, are not beholden to any outside organization, and do not depend on personal connections or past rulings to secure future business. Unlike administrative tribunals, their judges are not answerable to an executive authority in a position to replace them if dissatisfied with their rulings. Unlike specialized tribunals, they have no specific agenda to promote. Unlike private adjudicators, the salaries of their judges cost the litigants nothing. And if the federal government becomes convinced that state courts already in place have the capability to enforce expanding federal law, it will be reluctant to embark upon the massive court expansion that would be needed to enforce all new federal law exclusively in federal courts.

The critical factor is capability. If courts of general jurisdiction are to stay abreast of their competition and survive, they must become as competent as their competitors in providing "just, speedy, and inexpensive determination of every action," the goals of court reform expressed in Rule 1 of Federal Rules of Civil Procedure. The goals are clear, but the steps needed to reach these goals require radical change in customary practices of judges and lawyers in their dealings with one another. These changes are of two kinds: 1. Court reassertion of effective control over legal processes and fee awards; and 2. court insistence on lawyer accountability for wasteful tactics, abusive practices, and needless increases in the cost of litigation.

INCREASED COURT CONTROL OVER LEGAL PROCESSES AND FEE AWARDS

The almost universal prevalence of waste, duplication, and delay in the litigation process comes about because in every contested cause there is a minimum of two sides, and one side alone cannot control the process. In most cases one side wants the process moved along expeditiously, while the other prefers to see it delayed indefinitely. The ease with which delay can be achieved by a competent lawyer (who suffers no loss in prestige or standing at the bar by use of delaying or obstructive tactics) means that the side seeking speedy resolution of the cause can be frustrated indefinitely. Under prevailing legal structures cost-effectiveness in litigation depends on a collaborative effort by both sides to succeed; in lawyer jargon, "it takes two to tango." A defendant without any real defense may attempt to make the litigation so expensive the other side will be forced to settle. A plaintiff without a case may seek to keep the cause pending indefinitely in the hope something will turn up or it will be paid to go away. To further these objectives a lawyer may employ what are known as scorched-earth or take-no-prisoners tactics through whose use process devastates substance. Depositions continue for years; documents are sought by the roomful; answers to interrogatories are demanded by the thousands. In many instances lawyers on both sides are happy to accommodate each other in wasteful, sometimes useless procedures. Lawyers who are expected to tango may collaborate in a continuing tableau vivant that gives the illusion of movement where none exists. In these circumstances the sole remedy of a party seeking to make the litigation cost-effective is to persuade the court to exercise its coercive power to prevent waste and delay and make scorched-earth tactics unprofitable. But in past years such persuasion has borne little fruit.[9] Judges have generally left control over pre-trial activities to the lawyers and have accepted the invariable argument that grave injustice might result from any premature limitation of the issues or restriction on discovery. The easiest and safest course for the judge has been to let the game continue more or less unchecked, perhaps accompanied by some judicial exhortation of more bark than bite. Similar dilatory tactics have been tolerated in courtroom proceedings. If left uncontrolled, each phase of the trial—jury selection, examination and cross-examination of witnesses, argument of factual and legal points— can be protracted almost to kingdom come.

One example will illustrate. Under earlier procedures a witness's testimony was heard once, at the trial. Later rules allowed the testimony of a witness to be taken in advance of trial but almost invariably the same testimony was given again at trial. This duplication does not end the matter. In jury trials demand is often made that the judge first hear the testimony of an already-deposed witness in advance of his appearance before the jury in order to sanitize its content. As a result the same testimony may be given three times instead of once. Traditionally, the role of the judge throughout this process has been passive, like a boat at anchor always facing the prevailing wind and tide.

In their initial attempts at reform, state legislatures, as in California, sought to achieve court reform by a mechanical multiplication of procedural rules that specified in numbing detail a judge's ruling in every conceivable situation, with the result that the legal process became more complicated, dilatory, and costly than ever.[10] More recently, legislatures have begun to recognize that court reform will not be achieved by multiplying procedural rules that tie a judge's hands and continue his dependency on the collaboration of adversarial lawyers, but must come through active efforts of the judge who directs and controls the legal process. To an increasing degree judicial institutions and judges are being given authority to establish and enforce rules governing the use of legal processes.[11] This expansion of judicial authority is often accompanied by an increased answerability of judges for proper performance of their duties to judicial performance commissions, some of which have only a minority of judges and lawyers as members.[12]

Inevitably, such increased judicial authority and responsibility is requiring judges to retake control of the course of legal proceedings. To do so effectively against the resistance of one or more counsel, the judge must quickly master the essentials of a cause in order to control its progress and maintain its forward motion. The great trial judges, such as Charles E. Wyzanski Jr. in Boston, Leon R. Yankwich in Los Angeles, and Milton Pollack in New York, have been characterized by their ability and willingness to undertake this task.[13] This process is being made easier in multijudge courts in metropolitan areas, which, following the example of personnel assignment within large law firms, assign specialized types of causes to judges knowledgeable in the specialty involved, thereby facilitating judicial control of court proceedings as well as saving litigants the time and expense that would be needed to educate a judge unfamiliar with the specialty. The Los Angeles Superior Court now uses 15 different specialized areas for case assignment in its central district.[14]

In addition to more effective control over the conduct of legal proceedings, judges are taking a closer look at fee applications and exercising greater initiative in determining the reasonable value and need for the services for which fees are sought, particularly in common-fund causes, where fees are directly charged against the interests of the beneficiaries. To an increasing degree judges assume a fiduciary role on behalf of beneficiaries in evaluating the usefulness of the services rendered. In taking this closer look judges are returning to first principles: What has been the value of the services to the client or beneficiary? What is a reasonable charge for the services performed? With these queries they bring a breath of fresh air into the artificial world of fees based on lawyer-time spent. Judge Milton Pollack, an experienced trial lawyer before he became a judge, summarized the essentials of fee awards in a few cogent paragraphs:

The meter method tends to disregard the fact that a fee for legal services must also bear a proper relationship to the value of the engagement to the client, the amount involved and the importance of the services required. The requirement that time records be kept by counsel seeking compensation through the courts was initiated as a check against runaway charges on the upside and . . . unrestrained fee demands. . . . [It] was not an invitation for the distortion of the value of the required services or the proliferation of unnecessary unwarranted activity. . . .

It is possible to spend an enormous amount of time on relatively and objectively trivial and inconsequential matter either through a failure to appreciate the overall place in the total engagement of a particular segment, or through lack of basic fundamental knowledge of the subject matter. . . . Consequently, before the meter is allowed to sweep the costs out of proportion to the subject matter it is incumbent on counsel to discriminately select his activities consistent with the requirements of an engagement, but with a realistic awareness that a case may not be worth what the meter will tally up to if left to run without restraint.

Judge Pollack then concluded that the fee application of Morgan Stanley's counsel had departed from reality to an inordinate degree and reduced the fee to a quarter of the amount sought.[15]

As a further development of this closer look at fee applications, judges are reexamining the two mechanical standards heretofore alternatively used for fee awards: self-reported time spent multiplied by a self-declared hourly rate; and an appropriate percentage of the recovery, gross or net. More and more judges are beginning to employ variations of both standards as cross-checks in order to arrive at suitable fees.[16] Many are also beginning to disallow costs claimed for secretarial overtime, for work done by librarians, clerical personnel, and other support staff (viewing these expenses as part of a lawyer's overhead),[17] to disallow fees for excessive internal lawyer conferences, and to view with skepticism fee applications for double-digit hourly work days.[18]

Collectively these critical looks are producing substantial fee reductions, which include the Pfizer heart-valve implant case, in which fees of $33 million were sought and $11.25 million awarded; the General Motors fuel-tank case, in which a fee award of $9.5 million was reversed on appeal with the suggestion that $3.2 million might be more than enough; and the hospital-photocopy reimbursement case, in which fees of $5.6 million were sought and $2 million awarded.[19] In making fee determinations, judges are now receiving assistance from nonprofit consumer advocacy groups, which formally appear in court to oppose lawyer applications for fees that appear excessive. Ironically, the same lawyers who pride themselves as public protectors of consumer interests turn with fury on other public-interest groups that seek to protect consumer interests by monitoring lawyer applications for fees.[20]

COURT INSISTENCE ON LAWYER ACCOUNTABILITY

To be effective, judicial control of lawyers and litigants in court and in their use of legal process requires authority to sanction lawyers and litigants who resort to abusive practices. Just as enforcement of court orders and subpoenas requires the ultimate sanction of arrest and as maintenance of order in court requires the ultimate sanction of contempt, so lawyers who have been given exclusive privileges to initiate legal process and represent litigants in court are beginning to be held accountable for abuse of their privileges. New controls give judges the power to sanction both litigants and their lawyers for improper conduct. In California, both federal and state law authorize courts to impose sanctions against a lawyer, his client, or both, for bad-faith tactics or frivolous claims.[21] As one might expect, these provisions have been strenuously resisted by substantial segments of the legal profession, which take the position that lawyers must remain free to advocate any position, fact or fiction, and may not be held responsible for errors or misrepresentations.

Undoubtedly, these new sanctions run counter to legal practices that have prevailed in this country for generations. Since Elizabethan days it has been said that a diplomat is an honest man sent abroad to lie for his country. In the twentieth century it could be said with equal validity that a lawyer is a person sent to court (or press conference) to lie for his client, and if not to lie to report as fact events that have not gone through the formality of having taken place. Yet today in a lawyer's direct dealings with the court (as contrasted with his activities outside the court) toleration of the common practice of lawyer distortion and misrepresentation without fear of serious consequences is rapidly eroding. Lawyers can be held responsible for lack of a good-faith justifiable belief in the accuracy of what they file and say in court and in their initiation and use of legal process. Yet progress comes slowly. On the morning of April 12, 1995, a prospective, as yet unstructured, hostile takeover bid for Chrysler Corporation was announced; by that afternoon 28 lawsuits had been filed in the Delaware courts in opposition to the terms of the prospective takeover.[22] Patently, the filers of the 28 lawsuits could not have made reasonable inquiry into the facts, in that the takeover proponents themselves had not yet formulated the specific content of their proposal.

Outside the courthouse judicial control over lawyers' activities in pending cases has been a different story. The difference arises from conflict between the ideal of freedom of speech and press (Pentagon Papers) and that of fair trial based on court testimony under oath and subject to cross-examination (*Sheppard v. Maxwell*).[23] The press excesses in *Sheppard* and other highly publicized trials in the 1960s highlighted this conflict and brought demands for stronger controls over lawyers and judicial proceedings in order to ensure fair trial. These demands produced specific rules of professional conduct designed to limit what lawyers could say about pending proceedings outside the courtroom and to proscribe out-of-court statements likely to materially prejudice the proceedings.[24] These rules, however, contained a massive loophole that allowed lawyers to make out-of-court statements to counter adverse publicity initiated by others. Even so, opposition by many lawyer groups and by all media groups to any limitations on out-of-court statements by lawyers remains intense, an opposition largely based on the constitutional right of lawyers to free speech. These groups argue that the First Amendment guarantees lawyers the right to talk anywhere, anytime, and on any occasion about pending legal proceedings, a right that may be limited only when a clear and present danger threatens continuance of the proceedings themselves. Since under the First Amendment the parties, their friends, relatives, and press agents can talk freely to the media, the argument goes, their lawyers are entitled to do the same.

Judicial views on the legality of restrictions on out-of-court lawyer statements were mixed, as illustrated by a later dissenting opinion of four justices of the Supreme Court, who concluded that absent a clear and present danger to the judicial process itself, a lawyer has a constitutional right to plead an indicted client's case "in the court of public opinion."[25] Because of this continuing opposition, trial judges were reluctant to issue restrictions, known as gag orders, on out-of-court statements by counsel, restrictions that not only were sure to antagonize the media but might also be set aside by a higher court as an unconstitutional interference with free speech. As a consequence the rules of professional conduct and administrative regulations designed to curb trial in the court of public opinion became largely ineffective. The prevailing custom has been to allow lawyers to speak about pending cases whenever, wherever, and to whomever they please. In practice a lawyer has been free to lie like a trooper to the media in vouching for the truth of his client's story and in launching accusations against others, a practice that fortifies the popular impression of a lawyer as the client's mouthpiece. Although such advocacy is practiced by all types of lawyers in all types of cases, ranging from rezoning to new drug approvals to, currently, tobacco litigation, its most conspicuous practitioners have been found in the ranks of criminal defense lawyers who seek through media appearances to substitute fictitious issues and facts for those relevant to the charges. Thus a criminal defense lawyer in McCarthyesque, accusatory tones: "I have delivered to the district attorney conclusive proof that the murder of which my client stands falsely accused was committed by (freedom militia) (Colombian drug dealers) (neo-Nazi skinheads) (Arab terrorists). He refuses to investigate this evidence because of (unwillingness to admit a mistake) (political pressures) (hidden payola) (racial bias)." A steady downpour of such charges in press conferences and media interviews, shifting from one theme to another as the occasion warrants, often drowns the evidence presented in the courtroom.

Today, however, these long-established habits and practices are being overtaken by events.

- In 1991 the Supreme Court upheld the constitutionality of a standard of "reasonable likelihood of material prejudice" as a basis for issuance of gag orders on out-of-court lawyer statements.[26]

- The ubiquitous presence of television has vastly enlarged the audience for such statements and substantially increased the possibility that it may jeopardize a fair trial.

- Legislatures and appellate courts, dismayed by criminal trials that have become circus spectaculars, are pressing bar associations to strengthen ethical rules that would limit lawyer out-of-court discussions with the media about pending court proceedings.[27]

- The reasoning that equates lawyers' free speech with that of clients and their supporters is now viewed as inapplicable, in that it ignores the special position of the lawyer as an officer and functionary of the court who is privileged to act on behalf of the court in many matters but who also owes special duties to the court, among them truth and candor. The client, of course, seeks the cachet that comes with authentication of his story by an officer of the court, a service that more and more clients now expect the lawyer to provide as part of his engagement. Yet lawyers cannot function in diametrically opposing ways. They cannot use their special position to lie for their clients outside the courtroom without compromising the believability of what they say in court. It is a melancholy development in current legal practice that most judges now require factual assertions of lawyers to be made in writing under oath, and in critical matters may require the lawyer to be sworn as a witness and undergo cross-examination.

For these several reasons judges are beginning to hold lawyers to professional standards of conduct for what they say and do outside the courthouse, and gag orders are being issued more frequently.[28] We can expect increasing judicial pressures to ensure that cases are tried in court and not in kangaroo media presentations. A byproduct of this change is that the removal of client pressures on lawyers to lie for them at press conferences and in media appearances will help restore credibility to a profession that badly needs it.

To sum up, judges, in response to both external and internal pressures, are beginning to take a more active part in controlling legal processes and lawyers in order to make the proceedings less wasteful of litigant time and money and less susceptible to lawyer or client manipulation. This new judicial activism will directly affect legal fees (the principal component of legal expenses) in that less wasteful or misdirected time spent in the legal process means fewer billable hours, fewer fees for unprofessional and unnecessary services, and lower overall legal costs for clients.

13

Third Challenge: The Bite of Competition

With over 800 large law offices in existence where once there had been 12, sharply increased competition among them arrived. The average large law firm found itself ill-equipped for the rigors of this competition, in that it had become hostage to a large overhead requiring the constant nourishment of billable hours, to inflated earnings expectations of its lawyers, and in some instances to the need for continuous growth to maintain its profits and position. The principal causes of its predicament were its toleration of duplication, waste, and inefficiency, its custom of charging premium prices for all types of legal work regardless of benefits to the client, and its delivery in many instances of a mediocre product at a premium price. Heretofore, clients had put up with these practices on the assumption that nobody can do much about the weather or the cost of quality legal services. But under the changing atmospherics in lawyer-client relationships, clients began to bargain for prices that reflected current market conditions. On the demand side of this relationship, increased client sophistication and the rise in the legal world of corporate general counsel began to make themselves felt. On the supply side (i.e., availability of legal services), the explosive growth in the number and size of large law firms, accompanied by an aggressive extension of their operations into multiple metropolitan localities, increased the availability of quality legal services in a given locality from one or two firms to a large number headquartered both inside and outside the locality.

This mobility of legal services is new. For example, at the turn of the century legal matters stemming from maritime disasters in Hawaii or Alaska were handled by lawyers based in those areas. Today, maritime or aviation disasters occurring in Hawaii or Alaska may be handled by lawyers operating out of San Francisco, Los Angeles, Seattle, or Houston, with local counsel serving only in a standby capacity. Large law firm availability has become nationwide, in many instances worldwide. But enhanced availability brings enhanced competition as these firms expand into one another's territory. A large law firm no longer operates as a semi-monopoly in a given area but now competes with many rivals. Major securities-issuance work, once the exclusive preserve of New York law firms, is now common among law firms headquartered in Chicago, San Francisco, Los Angeles, and Houston. The result of this rapid increase in the number, size, and mobility of large law firms was an overcapacity in which supply outstripped demand for premium-priced legal services. As estimated by Steven Brill, editor of *The American Lawyer*, excess capacity in 1993 was as much as a third of existing capacity.[1] Inevitably, this oversupply gave all large law firms a powerful incentive to reorganize their operations to remain competitive with their rivals. Competition also intensified between large law firms and the growing in-house law departments of their clients, between large law firms and small law firms, and between large law firms and purveyors of specialized services who are not lawyers. In this sustained competition the critical element is quality as related to price, and to survive and prosper legal entities must become cost-effective.

The first major step to keep the large law firm competitive is elimination of bloated overhead and chronic extravagance. During the decades when delivery of legal services of all kinds to large organizations became immensely profitable, display of luxury by large law firms became an outward symbol of professional success. Yet conspicuous consumption and ostentatious spending is a relatively recent law firm development, one the original corporate law firms in the early years of the century had not needed to achieve wealth and standing. Consider offices. In 1935 Squire Sanders, then the largest corporate law firm in Cleveland, operated with a modest reception room, two medium-sized offices for its two most senior members, and 9-by-12-foot offices for all other lawyers, some still equipped with roll-top desks at a time such desks had not yet become collectors' items. But in time the temptation of luxurious surroundings (whose costs were tax-deductible as a business expense) overcame initial frugality and proved irresistible for almost all leading law firms. The story is told of a senior partner at Sullivan

& Cromwell, who, proudly showing his western client the new reception rooms, complete with deep carpeting, leather easy chairs, Oriental scatter rugs, walnut paneling, oil portraits of the firm's founders, and the founders' original partnership agreement encased in glass like the Declaration of Independence, all climaxed by an impressive circular stairway leading to the floor above, asked the out-of-towner what he thought. "I'll have a drink," was the reply, "but I won't go upstairs."

In today's large law firm, elegant decor, paneled offices for seniors, impressive conference rooms, private dining rooms, and art collections have become standard equipage.[2] Forgotten is the fact that conspicuous consumption and ostentatious display of wealth may scare away as many clients as they attract. Also forgotten is that such display encourages additional competition. Many new law firms were organized to compete with existing firms for premium business. Many of the organizers of these firms concluded that success depends on prestige and that prestige can be acquired through the trappings of success, much as the ancient Roman jurisconsults clad themselves in the most expensive robes of Tyrian purple to advertise their ostensible success. Through the magic of bank loans and easy credit it was no problem for a newly-organized firm to acquire these trappings. In law firms, both new and old, extravagance in office decor was matched by extravagance in travel (first class), in food and lodging (five star), in entertainment (skybox or ringside), and in office personnel (executive secretaries). Some of these firms resembled Aesop's frog who would be an ox and blew himself up larger and larger until he burst. A number of them went bankrupt, to the dismay of their unpaid creditors, who might face the problem of liquidating the firm's $3 million art collection in order to get paid. It is a safe prediction that in today's competitive climate, bloated overhead will be the first to go. It will be missed scarcely at all.

A second major step in achieving a competitive position, more difficult than elimination of waste in surroundings, is removal of waste and extravagance from the legal services themselves in a way that combines cost-effectiveness with product excellence, a step we identify under the familiar name *quality control.* There is no magic here, merely a painful series of adjustments and improvements, some large, some small, to ensure reliable delivery of quality services at competitive prices. One example of substantial savings in legal costs involves methods of recording court proceedings. Sixty years ago all court proceedings were recorded by shorthand reporter. Thirty years ago the stenotypist had displaced the shorthand reporter. Today, audiotape recording is becoming the predominant form of court reporting, with videotape lurking in the wings. In Los Angeles Superior Court audiotapes of a day in court may be obtained at the end of the day at a cost of about $40.[3] A daily written transcript of the day's proceedings costs about $1,200. Although use of the daily written transcript is in some respects more convenient, in areas such as contradiction of a witness or an opposing lawyer by his own words, audiotape is more useful. Yet most lawyers with solvent clients continue to order the costly, daily written transcript as a matter of routine. This is what we have always done, is their excuse.

The large law firm must keep asking itself three questions: How best can we serve the client's interest? How economically can we do the job? How can we ensure quality and remain competitive? In a competitive environment duplication and waste in the form of overstaffing, overloading, and overbilling will be early casualties. In trial work, the days of the medieval knight in full panoply, astride his armored war-horse, supported by squires, grooms, armorers, personal attendants, called out to battle on all but the most trifling disputes, will vanish or be limited to a few set engagements. The bulk of legal controversies will be handled by more agile infantrymen, operating singly or in pairs, lightly armed with personal computer, software programming, and communications equipment providing immediate access to legal and factual data banks at home base, all at a greatly reduced cost to the client. In office work and preparation of briefs and legal documents, there will be no need to compose a new treatise for each project. Electronic search of a law firm's data base and immediate access to outside collections of relevant information, including pertinent statutes and case law, enable the office lawyer to choose a suitable text from a wide selection in existing treatises, update its data for immediate client review through electronic communication, and deliver a faster and better product at a cheaper price as a result of the savings in secretarial, legal research, and library maintenance costs. Today, any activity, legal or otherwise, that consists largely of a repetitive application of rules is a target for automation. The client, a participant and collaborator in this process, will first welcome, thereafter expect, the savings in cost to be passed on to him in the form of lower fees. Two centuries ago James Watt identified his goal as that of "making engines *cheap*, as well as *good*."[4] To prosper, the large law firm must adopt the same objective, must change its primary goal from maximizing revenues and profit margins to one of maximizing client satisfaction through delivery of quality services that are cost-effective.

The information age has created powerful tools enabling lawyers to provide legal services that are cheap as well as good. A few firms, among them Kirkland & Ellis (Chicago) and Brobeck Phleger (San Francisco), have taken major steps to use technology to reduce client costs,[5] but most law firms have been slow to embrace this goal as a major objective. Judging from the professional literature of bar associations and related legal publications, the ideal of client satisfaction through delivery of a superior product at a lower price has made as yet little headway against that of maximizing sales and profit margins. The closest found to a change in viewpoint is a New York City Bar Association report outlining the huge savings in the cost of supplying legal services that can result from use of electronic data to process and retrieve legal and factual materials, but warning that these developments will put downward pressure on legal fees.[6] A state of mind that gives first priority to maximization of revenues and profits will ill-serve a law firm as the bite of competition deepens.[7]

The immediate consequence of these changes in the competitive environment may bring chaos to the pricing of legal services during a transitional period in which law firms struggle to maintain existing price structures while simultaneously yielding ground to clients who insist on price concessions. Prices for legal services may come to resemble air fares, where almost every passenger on a transcontinental flight pays a different fare. Alternatively, the airlines might adopt law firm billing methods for ticket pricing, a development visualized by Kevin Pratt in "What is the Air Fare from Denver to Chicago? Well it Depends. . . ."[8] Under this method an airline would charge a basic rate of $3 a minute from check-in time to luggage-retrieval time, adjustable by the passenger's income, occupation, business at destination, traffic delays, weather, the presence aboard of a copilot in training, and any use of computerized flight routing during the trip, the exact fare to be calculated two months later.

Chaos in the pricing of legal services, like chaos in airfares, does not mean that all legal fees will move in the same direction or that different types of legal services moving in the same direction will move at the same rate. Neither will all lawyers and all law firms face reductions in income. Premium fees will continue to be paid to individual lawyers and to a handful of law firms whose services are, or are thought to be, unique. Frank J. Hogan, counsel for billionaire Andrew W. Mellon in a criminal tax-evasion case, reportedly once said that the best client is a rich man who is scared. Today we would say the best client is a multinational facing disaster. In critical matters such clients will continue to pay premium prices for legal services they believe are unique, and the lawyers and handful of law firms rendering these services will continue to grow rich. But the overwhelming bulk of legal services does not fall within this category, and where a number of suppliers can perform legal services of similar quality, price competition will take hold. Implicit in this development is a general averaging down of competitive prices for routine legal services, even when the services are performed by large law firms. In Steven Brill's words, "Clients are not willing to pay blue-chip prices for hours worked by non-blue-chip lawyers churning work on non-blue-chip matters."[9] Those most vulnerable to the new competition will be second-tier lawyers and beginners in large law firms. Equally affected will be firms that prove unable to adjust to change.

Business will flow to agile, cost-effective suppliers of legal services and away from those that are not.

The consequences of changes in large law firm fees extend far beyond the world of collective and organizational clients, in that, as discussed earlier, the large law firm is the pacemaker in fees and billing practices for the entire legal profession, the pacemaker other lawyers and law firms are happy to emulate. If pacemaker fees are $150 to $500 an hour, lawyers of comparable age and experience throughout the profession, regardless of the work they are doing, feel entitled to demand the same fees and use the same billing practices—particularly when someone other than their client is being asked to pick up the tab. Thus, an increased competition that lowers the fees charged by large law firms benefits clients of all other lawyers and law firms, who must adjust their fees to lower prevailing levels.

It is reasonably certain that these new competitive pressures will intensify the search by large law firms for new business and new areas into which to expand. It is unlikely these firms will reject potentially profitable business merely because it is novel or departs from current views of respectability. That mistake has been made at least twice in the past. In the 1920s a number of leading corporate law firms in New York all but abandoned their trial capabilities in favor of more profitable office work. They later found it most difficult to rebuild trial expertise. In the 1950s, a new type of legal business arose, that of facilitating hostile takeovers of publicly-held corporations. The established firms spurned such work as not quite respectable, *infra dig*, apt to upset their existing clienteles. As a result, this immensely profitable new business gravitated to other lawyers, who not only became rich but were able to found legal empires of their own that now compete with the older firms in all areas of legal practice. The New York firm of Skadden Arps and the specialty firm of Wachtell Lipton are living memorials of this abdication by the legal establishment. Today, however, large law firm inhibitions against undertaking legal activities that promise profitability have disappeared. Whenever large amounts of money are involved, the entrance of these firms into causes of every kind—criminal defense, product liability, personal injury, or employment claims—is easy to predict. The federal judge supervising the breast-implant litigation in Alabama said of a proposed $4.25 billion settlement that he hoped to limit lawyers' fees and expenses to $1.01 billion.[10] Few firms, large or small, are likely to leave money like that lying on the table.

The new aggressiveness of large law firms in search of additional business will adversely affect many of the small firms of the northern hemisphere that specialize in a single legal activity (securities flotation, real estate development, etc.). Known as boutiques, some of them will continue to prosper as a consequence of the excellent reputation of their principals and the high degree of focus of their specialties, but the majority are vulnerable to invasion of their specialties by large law firms. Faced with these dangers, the boutique has a choice of several options, none of them good. It can attempt to metamorphose into a full-service large law firm as rapidly as possible by mergers with other boutiques. But while some mergers may be successful, the majority will not, because rapid growth from a small specialty base carries the multiple dangers of loss of quality and focus, of marriages made in haste to be repented at leisure. Or the boutique can make a series of publicized alliances with other boutiques possessing different specialties in order to offer in aggregate a full range of legal services. This course has all the dangers of merger, plus the added difficulty that no one is in charge. Like the Holy Roman Empire, loose alliances of separate boutiques remain aggregations of independent principalities, united only by a common letterhead. A third option, one increasingly used, is merger with an existing large law firm, thereby relinquishing identity and independence in return for a degree of economic security. A final option is to become the satellite of a large law firm that handles its same specialty, from which it receives those lesser matters the large law firm cannot or does not wish to handle. But dependency on the favor of another law firm is a position of high risk, one that can collapse overnight if the referring firm decides to handle such business itself. The one move that may be effective for the boutique is price discounting, but a large law firm on the prowl for business can also discount fees. For the small specialty firm, none of the available options offers reliable protection against the storm of competition now breaking over the profession.

Prospects in the southern legal hemisphere of individual, as opposed to collective, interests are equally bleak. As more and more routine legal services become targets of automation, fewer lawyers will be needed, and this shrinkage will press most heavily on the solo and small-firm lawyers of the southern hemisphere. Historically, these lawyers have relied on an occasional big strike to see them through a succession of dry holes. Now that their once undisputed territory is being vigorously prospected by large law firms and their most promising claims being jumped by formidable competitors, the odds against survival further lengthen.

In sum, intensified competition is already here, bringing with it casualties at all levels.

14

Fourth Challenge: Restlessness in the Workplace

A further challenge to the large law firm is the prevalence of job dissatisfaction among its lawyers, both junior and senior. Many juniors and lower-tier seniors see themselves as cogs in a machine operated by a handful of ranking seniors who exercise all real responsibility. The potentialities of these subalterns remain largely unknown because they have enjoyed few opportunities to develop and exercise their skills. Meanwhile, the firm remains apprehensive that its ranking seniors who exercise all major responsibilities may move elsewhere, leaving the firm to shift as best it can with untried, untested personnel. Clients have similar fears, and in some instances their worst fears have been realized.

The seeds of both problems were sown when corporate law firms began to concentrate exclusively on their profitable corporate work and treat other legal business, including trial work, as a distraction. When the corporate law firm evolved into the large law firm, typically it contained few lawyers competent to handle important trial work and found itself dependent on a handful of experienced trial lawyers, for whom it recruited squads of assistants known as litigators. These litigators, lacking experience in court and familiarity with responsibility, were ill-equipped to try cases, and if called upon to do so often delivered mediocre, or less than mediocre, performance.

The proper training of a trial lawyer is analogous to that of a commercial airplane pilot. A pilot on first acquiring his commercial license may start out with charter flights at some local airport, then progress to a commuter airline (first as copilot, then as pilot), then to short flights for a major airline (copilot, then pilot), and finally to transcontinental and international 747 flights (cocaptain, then captain). By the time he has become captain he has logged thousands of hours under every weather condition, encountered emergencies of all kinds, and been required to make countless responsible decisions on his own—experience a permanent subordinate officer on the 747 could never acquire no matter how many years he served. The experience needed by a trial lawyer is similar; he learns by doing. A variety of experience in dealing with judges, clients, witnesses, opposing counsel, enables the lawyer to handle himself to best advantage under adverse circumstances, which include obtuse judges, disingenuous clients, dishonest witnesses, and street-alley lawyers who knee, gouge, elbow, and otherwise disregard basic rules of personal and professional conduct. But for every dirty trick there is a counter, either immediate or delayed, through whose use an experienced lawyer can turn the situation to his ultimate advantage. A famous example is that of the McCarthy hearings, in which Boston lawyer Joseph L. Welch started Senator McCarthy's political destruction by his "Have you no sense of decency" speech directed at the senator during the latter's attacks on Welch's assistant. Not so well remembered is the timing of the speech, which Welch delayed to the thirtieth day of the hearings, by which time the senator's antics had become an embarrassment to his colleagues. Attempted earlier, the speech might have brought Welch a public reprimand or sanction.[1]

In law, as in acting, timing is essential, whether in trial work or in negotiation, and this sense of timing comes only from experience in doing, not from serving as another's assistant. Doing means carrying full responsibility for what is done, in that experience without responsibility is no more valuable than that acquired by investing on paper in the stock market. Trial lawyer development requires this type of on-the-job training, learning when to exploit successes, when to change tactics, when to cut losses. Law firm litigators who are not getting this training know it as well as anybody else and have good reason to be dissatisfied with their long-extended subordinate roles. With hindsight we can see that abandonment by the corporate law firm of the routine litigation that provided training and education for its young lawyers was an act of folly, one perpetuated by its successor, the large law firm.

The proper training of juniors is a task many law firms have either ignored or addressed in superficial fashion. Some firms, recognizing the limitations of subdivision and specialization but reluctant to make major changes, have attempted to forestall lawyer restlessness by assuring incoming lawyers of ample opportunity to volunteer for charitable or pro bono legal work at firm expense,[2] on the theory that this will allow juniors in the firm to exercise some independent responsibility and acquire the feeling they are handling work of importance. While pro bono work may provide a respite for the individual lawyer, four hours a week on legal aid or temporary full-time assignment to a pro bono program is not likely to give a junior the sense of responsibility he would acquire from representing real clients in a commercial context. Neither is such work likely to develop his skills in dealing with clients, in that charitable clients are not in a position to make demands or control the terms of the engagement and the progress of the case. Rather, pro bono work is somewhat like Lady Bountiful at the turn of the century ladling soup at a slum kitchen one morning a week and then returning to the comforts of her mansion and servants. Law firms must do better by providing opportunities for real work with real clients with representative problems.

In other efforts to address the problem of malaise, senior lawyers in large law firms at one time took squads of beginning lawyers to important conferences or to critical court proceedings, on the theory the juniors might learn something and would feel they were participants in matters of consequence. This practice was aided by the willingness of clients at that time to pay for services of little or no value to the client. But client willingness to pay for the education of juniors has become a historical curiosity, and because seniors know the cost of such excursions now comes out of their own pockets, these morale exercises have become rare. Beginning lawyers, like children on the family farm, are evolving from an income item into an expense item.

The most common training practice is assignment of real work to a junior, but work of limited scope that is directly supervised and funneled to the client through the senior. Important decisions and judgments remain the exclusive province of the senior, as do all critical contacts with the client. Disguised as it may be, this process tends to produce no more than specialized subordinates, highly skilled in specific techniques within a narrow range, experienced in carrying out directions of their superiors but wholly unaccustomed to making responsible decisions on their own. What is lacking in this process is development of the junior's ability to make hard decisions for which he assumes full responsibility. Such is the occupational weakness of the permanent bureaucrat, of the perennial Number Two whose growth has been stultified. More than anything else this subordinate status, divorced from ultimate responsibility, contributes to malaise within the large law firm. As Thucydides observed long ago, experience is learned in the school of danger and in those sudden crises which admit of little or no deliberation.[3]

In some firms a descending spiral of loyalty may develop between beginning and junior lawyers and the firm for which they work. Each year the mega law firm of 500 lawyers may hire a platoon of 50 to 70 beginning lawyers, who soon become aware that perhaps only a tenth of their number are destined to remain permanently with the firm.[4] Under leverage practices they will be replaced over the years by other beginners employed at lesser salaries. Many also discover they are not acquiring the experience needed to become fully-developed lawyers in possession of readily-marketable skills. Necessarily, the beginning or junior lawyer keeps a weather eye out for other berths likely to provide better professional development and prospects, and if he finds one he may jump ship. In turn, the firm, knowing of these possibilities, has little incentive to spend its resources to train and develop a lawyer who may soon leave after getting the benefit of an expensive training program. Lack of full professional development leads to lack of employee loyalty, and lack of employee loyalty may lead to minimization of firm training activities. Thus the descending spiral of loyalty.

Personnel problems within the large law firm are not limited to junior malaise but extend to renewal of its leadership and retention and replenishment of its senior ranks. Law firm leadership requires strong generalists who have transcended the narrowness of legal specialties and acquired both the ability to evaluate problems in full perspective and the skills to put their evaluations into operation. A familiar phenomenon of today is the law firm, dominated for years by two or three individuals, that collapses for want of leadership on the departure of its chief principals. At one time corporate law firms in need of leaders could rely on finding generalists to lead their firms from the ranks of lawyers with small-town legal experience, whose most promising members would move to wider spheres like baseball players moving from the minors to the big leagues. Thus, John W. Davis started his legal career in Clarksville, West Virginia, Thurman W. Arnold in Laramie, Wyoming, Wendell Willkie in Muncie, Indiana, Newton D. Baker in Martinsburg, West Virginia, and among lawyers heading the largest law offices of the government, Robert H. Jackson in Jamestown, New York, and Stanley F. Reed in Maysville, Kentucky. The early responsibility exercised by these lawyers in minor settings enabled them to advance to greater things. Today the raw material needed to provide such training is no longer available in small towns, where the sole remaining springboard for lawyers has become politics, an activity whose skills are not readily transmutable into those needed for law firm leadership. Leaders must be found elsewhere, either within the firm itself or in other law offices, public or private, operating in a metropolitan milieu. Internal leadership development is not a crop of spontaneous growth, but one that requires careful cultivation. The alternative, leadership from outside the firm, often constitutes a speculation on reputation and not on observation.

The problem of renewal also exists in replenishment of a law firm's senior ranks. Top-flight trial lawyers now rarely move from Urbana, Ohio, to Cleveland to New York, as did George Eichelberger in the 1920s, or from Porterville, California, to Los Angeles, as did Guy Knupp in the 1930s. Movement today is between metropolitan areas, New York to Los Angeles, Cleveland to Dallas, San Francisco to Washington, Chicago to Houston, or from one law firm to another in the same metropolis. The makeshift solution adopted by many large law firms for replenishment of their senior ranks or expansion into new specialties has been to recruit needed senior lawyers from other metropolitan law firms, or from government law offices, a process known as lateral hiring. These lateral movements among large law firms and from government to private offices—a traffic that has created a proliferation of lawyer-search firms—present distinctive problems of their own. The new lawyer may be unknown to the firm except by reputation, which may turn out to be skim milk masquerading as cream, and the firm may be unfamiliar to the new lawyer, who does not know its standards, internal workings, or ways of doing business. Lawyers within the firm may resent the new arrival, and issues of comparative compensation may fester. Thus, a senior coming into a large law firm from another office presents a gamble by both senior and firm on quality, fit, and contentment. And when, as now often happens, groups of lawyers, even entire departments transfer from one firm to another, the gamble is for higher stakes at longer odds. For senior lawyers the positive side of legal specialization lies in this new freedom to move from one firm to another when their specialty is flourishing. For example, in boom times real estate development lawyers who generate large fees for a law firm may become dissatisfied with their share of profits at firm A and move as a group to firm B, which promises them more. But in today's legal world the town mouse who feasts on the best of cheese lives in the ever-present shadow of the cat. Real estate has busts as well as booms, and when bust arrives firm B may no longer be willing to pay premium compensation to its new real estate lawyers, but instead may cut them adrift. All such lateral movements should be clearly understood by the parties as involving "Explosive Materials, Handle with Extreme Care."

This lateral mobility is a great breeder of lawsuits among lawyers and law firms, and each move may generate a new lawsuit.[5] Its more lasting vice is that it fosters continuing instability and decreasing professionalism in legal organizations of all sizes by nurturing a culture of mistrust under which each lawyer becomes primarily concerned with her personal interests and prospects rather than those of the law firm and fears that rival colleagues may invade what she considers her preserve.[6] She organizes her work to give herself exclusive access to existing and potential clients, even though others in the firm could handle particular items of work more effectively. The ever-present possibilities of lateral movement tend to distract senior lawyers from their real business of representing clients to the best of the firm's collective abilities into time-consuming jousts within the firm over personal status and earnings. Its consequence is to make the cost of legal services for the client higher than it would be under a stable regime in which the client's interest remained paramount.

In sum, the large law firm may have chronic personnel problems at all levels of its operations. For the most part it has not squarely faced these problems of job dissatisfaction and leadership development.

15

The Shape of Law Firms to Come: Professional Management

The large law firm of today is a powerful, effective, but imperfect vehicle possessing structural flaws that arise from its own strengths. To ensure its continued existence it must respond to the four major challenges previously discussed. In many respects its problems are similar to those of business organizations in the early years of the Industrial Revolution, which found themselves plagued with problems of shoddy work on the disappearance of guild controls, with problems of dishonest dealings in the marketplace as the importance of personal relationships declined, with problems of increased competition resulting from exponential increases in production, and with a restive labor force unhappy with its subdivision of task and insecurity of employment. Law firm problems are also comparable to the contemporary problems of universities and health-care institutions, many of which, according to Henry Chauncey Jr. of Yale's Department of Public Health, have failed to police themselves, failed to manage their institutions well, failed to listen to those who use their services, and, worst of all, grown arrogant in the process. These failures Chauncey attributes to an unwillingness to recognize that they are now large organizations.[1] We have seen the need for large law firms to address their similar problems. While the initial response of lawyers, law firms, and bar associations was that nothing was wrong in this best of all possible legal worlds, ritual denial has largely run its course. Perceptive members of the profession no longer seriously dispute the need to respond to these challenges. The debate now centers on appropriate responses that will bring inconsistent objectives into harmonious balance: tighter control of lawyer activity with greater exercise of lawyer responsibility; maintenance of quality with competitive pricing; and job satisfaction with specialization and collaborative work.

Yet before a large law firm can grapple with these problems, it must put its own house in order by creating a management structure capable of carrying out the policies it adopts. Like Topsy, law firms have just growed, spreading from city to suburb, city to city, state to state, country to country, in a megalopolitan sprawl so rapid that effective control has been left behind. When leading law firms were relatively small (20 to 40 lawyers) one person could be familiar with everything of importance going on in the office, set its standards, make them stick, and still find time to practice law. But as the size of firms continued to grow, the assumption that a ranking senior could keep an eye on firm affairs while continuing to practice law full time became strained when the firm's size exceeded 50 lawyers and wholly shattered as its size increased to 200, 400, 600, 1,000, or more lawyers. These firms initially thought that a managing partner (without too much authority) would satisfy, and lawyers were designated to assume that post, often selected for availability and not for managerial talents and leadership skills. Availability frequently meant someone not overburdened with clients, someone whose clients could be readily serviced by others, or someone nearing retirement age. As the size of law firms continued to grow, boards of directors or executive committees were created to assist the managing partner, boards usually consisting of working seniors who continued to practice law full time. With further growth, some breakdown of the firm's mass of lawyers into groups became necessary, either by function (trial lawyers, tax lawyers, etc.), by location (Los Angeles, San Diego, Palo Alto), by client assignment, or by task force. The heads of these groups, usually the most senior lawyer within the group, functioned in this capacity in addition to their activities as practicing lawyers.

Such a loose system often proved a ticket to disaster, with amateur managers and part-time group heads unsuccessfully attempting to control activities of the prima donnas of the firm who were bringing in large profits. And amateur management often allowed the rivalries that develop in any sizable organization to escalate into feuds and factions. Yet despite the demonstrated defects of amateur management, a powerful rear-guard of senior lawyers continues to resist changes that would lead to effective control over its activities and continues to view the functions of a managing partner or governing board as no more than those of office management. These seniors, often unwilling to recognize that they are now members of a large complex organization and to identify their own financial success and well-being as products of the health of their organization, wish to eat their cake and have it, too—to enjoy all benefits of membership in a large organization and at the same time remain free to act independently as their personal interests and inclinations dictate. This attitude resists any elevation in the status and authority of a managing partner to that of firm leader and expresses itself in the disdainful question: Why would anybody want to manage a law firm?[2]

Today's law firm management faces not only the problems of the Industrial Revolution and the Information Revolution, but additionally the problems of the Management Revolution. The latter tag is more than empty rhetoric invented by management consultants to market their own services. In shorthand form it represents the necessity for every large organization to deal with the many problems inherent in the conduct of large-scale activities, problems that did not exist a generation or two earlier. A 600-lawyer law firm with a workforce of 1,500 faces most of the organizational problems of any large business corporation. Consider, for example, hiring and firing. In earlier times all employment not under specific contract was employment at will. An employer could hire and fire as it pleased, for any or no reason. Today, employment, promotion, demotion, and termination have become subject to a host of laws and government regulations, for example those that prohibit racial, religious, sex, age, and disability discrimination. Quotas or goals for specified groups may be pressed. Collective bargaining may be sought by particular groups of employees. Toleration of job-related sexual harassment is a serious offense that can cost a firm millions of dollars, as is firm interference with office romance.[3] Problems of mental health, repetitive stress, alcoholism, drug abuse, breaches of client confidentiality, and misuse of confidential information insistently intrude on law firm management.

Consider finances. The management of a law firm of 600 lawyers grossing $250 million a year must have accurate information about its present and future finances, its cash flow, its accounts receivable, the cost and profitability of its various work segments, and the value of its services to its clients. To make sound decisions on firm commitments for future expenses (lawyer employment, long-term leases, investments in new locations) it must possess reliable working estimates of its business prospects, of the effect of changes in the general economy on its clients' affairs, and of the trends, up or down, of its major legal specialties and those of its competitors.

Finally, as the size of an organization grows, so does its diversity of opinion over objectives, strategies, and tactics, and so does the possibility of disagreement over allocation of resources and division of profits. For a large law firm to operate successfully over the years its management must possess sufficient political skills to broker competing demands and reconcile the disappointed. In short, law firms, like hospitals, universities, and other large service organizations, require effective, knowledgeable management by leaders who can organize, persuade, maintain or change course, and develop their successors. In times of rapid evolution, as at present, an organization particularly needs a skilled generalist as its leader, one who can go outside an existing dialectic that has become exhausted and take the organization in new directions.

Effective control over a large, widely-dispersed organization to ensure performance of its objectives is not a venture into unknown territory. Its elements include: a clear statement of mission and of acceptable and unacceptable conduct; skilled, responsible leadership with access to relevant facts and with the authority and will to take appropriate action as needed; and division of the organization into smaller manageable units, each in turn headed by a responsible, knowledgeable leader, able and willing to carry out the organization's objectives. There is no mystery here. A church, an army, a university, a political party, a symphony orchestra, divides its activities into component units of parish, company, department, precinct, and section. Each unit is small enough to enable its leader to know everything organizationally-relevant about each member of his unit—strengths, weaknesses, reliabilities, uncertainties. The best examples of large-organization management are found in service organizations that for centuries have successfully operated large entities with widely-dispersed units, such as an international church or a national army. The common pattern of these organizations is concentration of policy formulation and appointment of key personnel in a central headquarters under individual or small-group control, together with decentralization of operations into local organizations, each under a responsible leader, a bishop or a commanding officer, who is given general objectives and guidelines of acceptable conduct, who remains free to conduct his own operations, but who is held fully accountable for results, good or bad, within his diocese or command. The process combines centralized control over policy and key personnel with local autonomy over operations. Within each diocese or command a similar process is used for subunits: centralized control by the bishop or commanding officer over policy and key personnel, and decentralized operations under a parish priest or subordinate commander, who is accountable for results.

In the instance of a large law firm or similar personal-service group whose members need a degree of autonomy to function, effective management requires management of professional caliber, both for the organization as a whole and for its principal subdivisions. This does not necessarily mean a professional manager from outside the legal ranks. It means a manager who has demonstrated competency in running an organization, preferably but not necessarily within the firm itself, and who is willing to devote the time and energy needed to accomplish the task.

Before reviewing the needs of effective law firm management, some discussion of law firm structure is appropriate. Today's law firms are required by law to be owned and operated by lawyers. But law firms are free to select the corporate or the partnership form of doing business, a selection largely determined by tax considerations and exposure to liability for errors and omissions. The particular form of business organization adopted (whether the firm's senior lawyers are identified as partners or shareholders) has little to do with effective firm management, for it is the reality of policies and controls that determines a law firm's ability to solve problems of integrity, quality, competition, and job satisfaction.

The different structures that law firms have tried include:

- A single entity, wholly centralized, with common accounting, with all decisions on client engagement, client billing, employment, and profit-sharing controlled by a central body.

- A single entity with autonomous divisions but with common accounting and profit-sharing.

- A single entity with autonomous divisions, separate accounting, and separate profit-sharing.

- Multiple entities at the same location using a common name, with or without common accounting (i.e., concessions—the probate concession, the bankruptcy concession, etc.).

- Multiple entities with only partially common ownership, with separate accounting and separate profit-sharing (affiliates).

- Multiple entities of separate ownership in different locations, united only by common name (franchises).

- Joint ventures for particular locations (a Moscow office for separate law firms) or for particular projects (a class action).

- Extensive use of temporary employees (contract workers, legal consultants).

The main objective of each of these various structures is to preserve and protect the goodwill associated with the firm name and at the same time avoid the deadening effect of centralized decision on all matters. Many of these structures, such as affiliates, franchises, joint ventures, and temporary employees, have been tried with indifferent results, in that control over quality and integrity is often ineffective, and loose control invites abuses. Wholly-centralized control has also been tried, with results that are generally unsatisfactory over any extended period. Probably the most successful structure is one that follows the church-army pattern of a single entity with a central governing agency and autonomous units under fully responsible heads. But this need not always be the case. Concessions under a single roof may work out, as for example, in the large civil law firm that shelters an independently-operated white-collar crime unit, conveniently located on the premises for those of its clients who run afoul of the law. With hundreds of law firms operating multiple offices we can expect endless variations in the details of organization and structure, some following the exigencies of client needs and demands, some switching from one structure to another to meet changed conditions. But those firms that over time remain consistently successful will have arranged their affairs, one way or another, to meet the challenges of client demands, court demands, competition, and job satisfaction.

The mechanics of effective management require the manager, whether of the central organization or one of its subunits, to obtain as much first-hand information as possible about firm operations in order to make sound decisions, for if unaware of abuses and neglects he will be unable to correct them while still small and will discover them only after they have become major problems. But he needs the eyes and ears of others as well as his own, and in using their services he must walk a fine line between keeping well-informed and encouraging tale-bearers, toadies, and back-stabbers. The central manager must know each unit head well, and in turn each unit head must know the members of his group sufficiently well to foresee their reactions under various conditions. Which ones are the likely corner-cutters, the potential fee abusers, the credit stealers, the triflers with facts? And which are capable, conscientious, honest in money matters, easy to work with? A large law firm in possession of reliable, detailed knowledge of its personnel and operations can be run like the New York Yankees under Casey Stengel— the troublemakers, no matter how talented, soon were no longer wearing the Yankee pinstripes and had taken their troubles elsewhere.

Effective management also includes periodic evaluation of each major engagement within the law firm to see whether its handling complies with firm policies and meets firm standards. In the days of $50 million law-firm liability for the acts of one or two of its members in a distant office, such evaluation has become essential. Effective evaluation, like audits of accounts, must remain independent of the normal system of controls and serve as a check on the effectiveness of those controls. Such oversight requires the services of autonomous seniors outside the usual chain of command, who report directly to the governing body or head of the firm. Here the large law firm might take a page from the practices of the Department of Justice, which with over 90 regional law offices to supervise relies on periodic review of all activities within an individual office by an inspector general, and from the similar practices of the State Department, which uses officers of ambassadorial rank to periodically evaluate in depth all operations of a particular embassy or legation.

Law firm governance must remain largely divorced from earnings in that the most capable managers may not be the best earners, and vice versa. Just as the president of a university may earn less than the famous heart surgeon in the medical school, the Nobel Prize winner who heads its research institute, and its successful football coach, so the manager and unit heads in a law firm must possess authority to control the conduct of all persons for whose conduct they are answerable, regardless of age and earning capabilities. For purposes of integrity control (honesty), earning capacity must be wholly disregarded, and for purposes of quality control (cost-effectiveness and excellence of work) it must be disregarded much of the time. Events of the past decade have shown that separation of management from earning capacity is essential to the long-term health of the large law firm, in that once a law firm gives money-making priority over other values, it has lost full control of its operations.

It can be argued that any system of centralized control merely creates an additional multilayered bureaucracy, and to some extent this is true. But consider the alternatives. A mega law firm doesn't run itself and won't avoid trouble for long if its lawyers are free to go their separate ways. With large organization comes the possibility of large mischief, and effective control is the tax the organization must pay to achieve and maintain effectiveness as a group. A truly effective management will keep layers of management at a minimum and the number of persons engaged in management activities as small as circumstances will allow.

16

The Shape of Law Firms to Come:
Integrity and Quality Control

INTEGRITY CONTROL

But effective organization and control to what specific ends? The first and most fundamental must be integrity control, whose aims are both immediate and practical, long-range and moral. The practical aim is to avoid catastrophe, in that a law firm cannot expect to survive more than one or two $40 to $50 million liabilities, and today the conduct of a single lawyer can create such a liability for a firm. Examples include the misfortunes of Jones Day (Cleveland) for events in Phoenix and on another occasion for events in Los Angeles, of Paul Weiss (New York) for events in Miami, of Kaye Scholer (New York) for events in Phoenix, of Rogers & Wells (New York) for events in San Diego, of Blank Rome (Philadelphia) for events in Florida, of Venable Baetjer (Baltimore) for savings-and-loan matters.[1] When scandal arises, the first question always asked is how the firm could have been so careless as to allow the improper conduct to occur under its banner. Excuses pointing out the value of autonomy, the difficulties of supervising large numbers of professionals engaged in multitudinous activities, or the perfidy of clients who betray their lawyers' trust fall flat. Even when such an incident does not threaten firm survival, its disposition may consume enormous amounts of time (and money) that otherwise could have been spent by lawyers of the firm in practicing law. Equally injurious, the judgment and reputation of the firm come into serious question. Its clients ask themselves whether they should continue to entrust their affairs to a firm that cannot keep itself out of trouble. Such dangers form the nightmare of the head of every large law firm, a nightmare that periodically becomes a reality.

The long-range aim of integrity control must be to ensure honesty in dealings—with clients, with courts, in commitments to other counsel—as a given throughout the entire range of firm activities, great and small. Because the essence of a lawyer's function is to act for another, to represent that other with fidelity and when necessary put that other's interests ahead of his own, and because a law firm is an aggregation of individual lawyers, the firm must insist on candor and straightforwardness in all its lawyers' dealings. If a law firm compromises its integrity and thereby injures its reputation, it has damaged its principal stock in trade, damage that may take years to repair. The education a law firm gives its young lawyers might well be modeled on the ancient Persian curriculum, *to ride, to shoot, to tell the truth,* updated *to reason, to draft, to tell the truth.*[2] Such an education teaches in Persian fashion that a lie is disgraceful and aims to instill justifiable pride in integrity of conduct, a pride that sustains faithful performance in the face of great temptation.

In a lawyer's dealings with courts and in his commitments to opposing counsel, his word must possess the guinea stamp of certified quality. Anything less dissolves all claims to any special recognition of a privileged status in court or to special recognition as an officially-authorized representative of a client. In the nineteenth century when traders in the Far East and the Central Pacific wished to make a solemn binding oral commitment they did so on "Word of an Englishman." A firm must strive to have its oral representations and commitments accepted on the same basis—Word of a Lincoln & Herndon lawyer.

In a lawyer's dealings with his clients this integrity must be as close to absolute as the conduct of human affairs allows. It is a standard a law firm cannot compromise, one it must apply to every lawyer in the firm, no matter how elevated his position or how much business he brings in. For example, overcharges, even those promptly paid without client objection, when discovered must be returned immediately. In today's climate the temptation is to turn a deaf ear, to do nothing, and thereby tacitly condone conduct that stultifies the essence of a lawyer as the faithful agent of another. Such inaction is not a product of conscious decision but one that results from the new, excessive preoccupation with money and from the loss of control over law firm operations that frequently accompanies explosive growth. It is a puzzle why in today's better-educated, better-trained legal profession the litigation practices of large law firms have descended to the level of the criminal bar, rather than the other way around as we might expect. We can speculate that the views of some of the lawyers entering those firms during their period of mushroom growth from the mid-1960s on—views formed at a time of widespread academic acceptance of moral relativism, of value neutrality, and of plausible theories of law as a mere reflection of power relationships—weakened to some degree the former general acceptance of a strict standard of professional morality and provided plausible rationalization for questionable but profitable firm practices. Yet, morality aside, a law firm's toleration of corner-cutting to enhance profits carries the real risk of blurring within the firm the distinction between questionable practices and those that violate civil and criminal law. Insider securities trading and use of confidential information for personal gain provide examples of this danger. A law firm that tolerates dubious practices may create a climate that leads some of its employees to conclude that even criminal acts are passable, as long as the risk of detection is small and the violation is comparable to exaggerations or omissions on an income tax return. In recent years a number of law firms have been embarrassed on one or two occasions by revelations of insider trading by their employees, but one large law firm has been involved in a total of eight such violations.[3]

Much learned discussion circulates on whether the practice of law is a business or a profession. It is both. A lawyer must make money to stay in business, and to stay in practice he must remain true to the obligations of his profession. If he does not deal honestly with his clients, he has become a hollow man, a carnival huckster who views each customer as a rube to be gulled. The first and greatest objective of controls, therefore, must be to create institutional habits, disciplines, and morale that make integrity habitual throughout the law firm, a matter of duty and honor that each and every lawyer in the firm would be ashamed to betray. The shining example for law firm emulation is the turn-of-the-century Boston trustee, who managed other people's money and property at a time trust companies did not dominate this activity. These professional trustees operated under standards of absolute integrity and absolute devotion to the interests of their clients. Lawyers as fiduciaries must strive to do the same. These are far from impossible standards, and there are many large firms that appear to have succeeded in meeting them, among them Davis Polk (New York), Covington & Burling (Washington), Wilmer Cutler (Washington), to name a few. Yet the prevailing attitude in the legal profession toward overcharges, excessive fees, and demands for excessive fees remains one of broad tolerance. At present these acts are viewed as less than venial sins, and a law firm does not ordinarily lose face among its peers when such an event is publicized. Rather, the matter is viewed as an unfortunate incident that could happen to anyone—there but for the grace of God, etc. And courts, faced with instances of flagrant overcharges, rarely order forfeiture of fees, but instead merely reduce them to reasonable amounts. The perpetrator of overcharges suffers no more moral condemnation within the profession than does the equestrian who knocks off a bar or two in a jumping competition. The opposing lawyers' conduct that so outraged Mr. Pickwick in Mrs. Bardell's breach-of-promise suit against him was an object of professional admiration by Pickwick's own lawyers, who said of Dodson and Fogg, "sharp practice theirs," "capital men of business," "excellent ideas of effect."[4] But if the legal profession remains infinitely tolerant and forgiving of overcharges and is willing to view them as temporary aberrations accompanying an otherwise admirable aggressiveness, the more important audience of clients is not. It is from this quarter that peril for the law firm comes. It is to forestall such peril that recapture of integrity is imperative.

A related aspect of law firm integrity control is the need for the firm to keep advised of the substance of client activities on which it is working. The perils to a law firm presented by dishonest clients engaged in defrauding others continue to multiply. It was once accepted that lawyers, like the three brass monkeys who see no evil, hear no evil, speak no evil, were fully protected against liability for their clients' frauds so long as they did not actively participate in them. Today, when a lawyer has reason to suspect client misdeeds in a pending transaction on which the lawyer is working, he has a duty to speak out to prevent fraud and in some instances a duty of independent investigation to detect it. If he does not, the lawyer himself may become liable for his client's misdeeds. This viewpoint has been epitomized by Judge Stanley Sporkin, who asked in reference to the blatant fraud accompanying the Lincoln Savings collapse: Where were the outside accountants and lawyers when clearly improper transactions were being consummated? Why didn't any of them speak up?[5] Clients' requests to stretch the facts, clients' misrepresentations to the firm, and clients' lack of candor can no more be tolerated by a law firm today than can similar conduct within the firm. And for the same reason: Toleration may expose both the firm's reputation and its treasury to the perils of massive liability.

It is a common practice for businessmen with checkered pasts to seek to prop up some gamy promotion or questionable deal by engaging a reputable law firm at premium fees to handle its mechanics, thereby bringing a degree of authenticity to the proposed transaction. If the law firm carelessly accepts the engagement, in effect the businessman has bought the use of the firm's good name. All may go well, and the law firm's prestige may facilitate a deal to which no objection is ever voiced. But then again it may not. Sooner or later a law firm employed in a number of these deals will find itself the target of irate investors or lenders who have suffered losses. Again, law firm excuses tend to fall flat. A further drawback to careless acceptance of a sleazy client is that junior lawyers in the firm who are required to work on the affairs of such a client will either lower their own standards to accommodate those of the client or become unhappy with the position into which they have been thrust. Neither event bodes well for the health of the law firm. In instances of suspected client dishonesty the law firm's sole real protection is to reject or terminate its representation of the client, no matter how tempting the fee. For example, in the manipulated stock sale by National Student Marketing Corporation, the firm of Covington & Burling (Washington) terminated its representation of the company. It was succeeded by White & Case (New York), which carried the sale to its completion, to the firm's long-continued public embarrassment and financial cost.[6] A similar sequence occurred when Rogers & Wells (New York) terminated its representation of a savings-and-loan client and was succeeded by O'Melveny & Myers (Los Angeles), which thereafter found itself a defendant in a multimillion-dollar lawsuit brought by Federal Deposit Insurance Corporation, charging the law firm with negligence and breach of fiduciary duty.[7] For lawyers, and everyone else for that matter, the cost of lending one's good name to seedy conduct is too high, even if payment is long deferred. A law firm that negligently jeopardizes its integrity has mortgaged its soul to the devil, and sooner or later Old Scratch shows up to collect.

QUALITY CONTROL

Equally important to a law firm as integrity is quality, both in the legal services rendered and in their cost-effectiveness for the client. In the latter area a major shift in conventional law firm perspective is overdue. The essential question involved—How economically can we do a good job for the client?—stands in sharp contrast with the dominant question of recent years—What sort of fee can we charge?

When glorification of gross revenues and profit margins became paramount, whatever contributed to their augmentation was for the best. The dollar was crowned king. Extravagance in running up fees and costs became habitual in that a lawyer had little incentive to do otherwise. A major case from a solvent client comes into the office. The senior promptly assembles his juniors and says: "Half a dozen [or three dozen] of you better go to work on this right away."[8] The legal war machine goes into action before any objective is selected or campaign mapped, much as masses of infantry were deployed in World War I. Under the prevailing system of billable hours, which divorces fees from results, production is given priority over productivity. Such a flawed reaction results in much waste, for which the client pays. Too often, the lawyer forgets that by doing good for the client he will do well for himself.

The current system of perverse incentives (that is, longer hours bring bigger fees, quicker promotions, and greater profits) is a system that under normal workings of human nature all but guarantees abuses. Moreover, its basic premise may be questionable. At the turn of the century, a steelworker's daily shift at the mill was 12 hours. When the eight-hour day was first proposed and then later adopted, it was asserted that productivity would suffer. Nothing of the sort happened. Less time was wasted, and workers' activities became more focused. In legal circles today there is interest in a new approach known as *working smarter*,[9] one based on the premise that clients will find it advantageous to employ firms in which labor is smarter rather than firms in which it is cheaper. It may be that an imaginative quality control will demonstrate that shorter working days by lawyers result in increased productivity, in which event massive billable hours will become a sign of inefficiency. It may also be that *working smarter* can produce both increased earnings for lawyers and lower total legal costs for clients, thereby reforging the link between superior product at a premium price and lower total client costs, the link that was broken when the corporate law firm evolved into the large law firm.

The long-overdue severance of fees charged from time spent, followed by more fixed arrangements (flat fees, flat fees for specific segments of a continuing project, incentive contracts, fees based wholly or partially on results), will put lawyer-client relationships on a firmer footing in respect to fees. Under such arrangements a client knows in advance what his legal costs in any given matter are likely to be and knows that lawyer-time spent will be the sole concern of the lawyer. Lawyers will continue to record their time, but their recording will be for internal firm purposes—to compare effectiveness among lawyers, to determine relative profitability of various employments, to use in bidding for future legal business. Within the firm the lawyer who does the job effectively with the least time wasted will advance to greater tasks and increased rewards. Under the changeover from billable hours to fixed arrangements, both law firm and client must focus at the outset on the expected duration of the project, its cost, and its probable outcome. This initial focus is sure to reduce the number of lawyer-client fee disputes that arise subsequent to employment, in that both parties will have realistically evaluated the project at its inception rather than after an expenditure of much effort and money. In making its initial evaluation the law firm must estimate the worth and cost of the project on incomplete information, much as a highway contractor does when full geological information is not available. The law firm, drawing on experience, will provide in advance for unexpected adverse developments. The client will do the same. The result is specific agreement on fees, subject to modification for specified contingencies. The development of legal-estimator specialists to perform these functions is probable.[10]

Thus far our discussion of law firm quality control has dwelt more on cost-effectiveness than on excellence of the services themselves in court, at the negotiating table, and in the office. How can a large law firm ensure the quality of legal services rendered daily by its hundreds of lawyers? The answer includes proper organization, supervision, and training of its lawyers as previously discussed, but it also requires something more—periodic independent evaluation of the quality of the law firm's services. We have previously referred to the use of a senior lawyer to aid the firm on issues of integrity. That same senior can also serve as an autonomous evaluator of the quality of the services rendered to clients by conducting, outside the chain of command, an independent examination of the handling of specific operations. From firm files and discussions with the lawyers involved, he evaluates the effectiveness of the firm's engagement: strategy and tactics, cost to the client in relation to stakes involved, results obtained. Next, he discusses the representation with the client and its personnel: Were they pleased with the services and results? Did they like the lawyers working on the engagement? Did they find the fees satisfactory? What can the law firm do to serve the client better? A skilled senior will soon unearth latent client discontent or resentment. His report to management may confirm the firm's impression that relations with its client are on track, or it may indicate a need for change. No good reason exists why such reviews should not be routine or why they should upset normal operations of a law firm. Corporations have their auditors, hospitals their review committees, universities their oversight committees, and businesses their management consultants. Each benefits from the salutary effect of periodic third-party review of its operations. Large law firms can profit from similar oversight.

A few firms have made tentative moves in this direction[11] but most still look on independent review as somehow unprofessional. Yet the alternative to periodic, independent evaluation of a law firm's major operations may be the unexpected discovery one day that a million-dollar-a-year client has taken its business to a competitor down the street. Many clients, perhaps most, do not enjoy confrontations or hard bargaining with their own lawyers. If, after a few discreet demurs to the size of the fees, the quality of the work, or the need for specific services, their reservations are not satisfactorily dealt with, they move elsewhere. Such a move may often come as a complete surprise to an uninformed law firm management. If nothing else, the wisdom of having a fully-informed management with greater knowledge of client relationships than that filtered through billing seniors is a matter of enlightened self-interest, comparable in value to an annual physical checkup.

17

The Shape of Law Firms to Come: Competitiveness and Job Satisfaction

COMPETITIVENESS

Creation of a well-managed legal organization that functions as the soul of integrity and provides quality services avails nothing unless the large law firm is able to operate profitably in a competitive environment. Competition in legal services, as in commerce, keeps prices within bounds and gives producers a powerful incentive to work more efficiently. In areas where legal services are easily duplicated by others, price competition is steadily intensifying, and reductions in fees for such services are inevitable. This brings us to the subjects of law firm production costs and sales costs. To remain profitable under a regime of reduced fees, a firm must lower both. We have previously discussed the need for the large law firm to reduce its general costs by eliminating extravagance, by economical lawyering that avoids duplicative services, by full use of the economies of specialization, and by automation. But more will be needed to operate profitably in a highly competitive environment. The large law firm must become a low-cost producer. To identify the problem is easy, to put a solution in place most painful.

COMPETITIVENESS: PRODUCTION COSTS

A full-service law firm is an aggregation of mutually reinforcing departments that require different levels of skill, that face different degrees of competition, and that deal with fluctuating demands for their particular services. It is in the firm's interest to keep all departments in good health, even during a severe downturn in a particular department's business, "for," in Kipling's phrase, "the strength of the pack is the wolf, and the strength of the wolf is the pack." In practical terms this means that at times certain departments need to be subsidized by those that are temporarily more prosperous. Fair enough. But subsidization has its limits, and a department whose work is consistently less profitable than others cannot expect subsidies indefinitely. Profitability of a department is largely determined by the amounts it can charge for its services, and these amounts depend on the stakes involved, the rarity of the skills involved, and the number of competitors offering similar services. Many lawyers are fully qualified to draw wills or sue on insurance policies; fewer are qualified to handle a tax-free exchange of securities in a corporate consolidation or pursue a major software infringement action; fewer still to handle a multistate bank merger. These differences suggest that profitability of different departments within a large law firm varies widely, and the textbook examples of law firm accounting practices bear this out.[1]

The major element in a department's cost of producing legal services is the compensation paid to the lawyers who perform these services. Yet historically the large law firm has been structured to provide roughly comparable earnings for lawyers of comparable age and experience, regardless of profitability of their departments or the type of business on which they work. In past years firms attempted to equalize profitability among departments by charging premium prices for relatively routine services, will-drafting for example, but clients today insist on competitive prices for such work, without which they may take it and other more substantial business elsewhere. To retain its clientele, a farsighted firm must charge market prices in all departments—premium prices where its services excel, competitive prices where its services are easily duplicated. The result is different charges for different categories of legal work, each fixed by intensity of competition, that is, market demand and available supply. Some indication of this change is beginning to appear in law firm directories that show firms listing different charges for different areas of work. As John Larson of Brobeck Phleger (San Francisco) noted, different categories of work require different pricing, different people, and different career paths. A client doesn't want to pay "Cadillac prices for Chevrolet work."[2] Inevitably, this means that lockstep compensation for lawyers in a firm will go the way of billable hours, as large law firms regroup to remain competitive in all areas of practice. Some subsidies of departments in highly competitive areas will continue in order to maintain the firm's status as a full-service law firm, the alternative being withdrawal from areas in which it does not excel and loss of status as a full-service law firm. Other subsidies will allow representation of prestigious clients (an art museum, a high government official, a famous foundation), and still others will preserve a desired presence (our Tokyo office). Yet lawyers engaged in subsidized or low-profit activities cannot expect the same earnings as lawyers engaged in highly profitable activities. Variations in fees charged by different departments within the same law firm bring about variations in earnings of comparable lawyers working in different departments. Lawyers in a routine department that cannot charge more than competitive fees must reconcile themselves to lesser earnings than lawyers in a department that provides unique services and charges premium fees. To the extent that fees fluctuate to meet competition, so will the earnings of individual lawyers. The lawyer whose services are overpriced in the market must lower her fees and thereby lower her earnings, and the lawyer whose services are underpriced relative to demand will insist on increased fees to make her earnings reflect her popularity. It is the same with departments. Periodic repricing will produce something akin to a true market.

Price competitiveness most quickly appears in fees for routine legal services and for services of beginning lawyers. As large law firms begin to charge competitive prices for these services, we can anticipate a general reduction throughout the entire profession of charges for such services. We can also expect starting salaries in large law firms to begin a relative decline when these salaries no longer produce income for the firm but have become a firm expense. Not even senior lawyers who possess prized legal skills are wholly exempt from the rigors of price competition, in that unique legal skills often become widely dispersed in a relatively short time, and specialties evolve into commodities. As this occurs, the price of these services falls, as has happened in tax law, securities law, antitrust law, and other once-esoteric specialties. The large law firm must also anticipate competition from nonlawyer organizations in areas that have become routinized. The pattern of the past is that as a particular type of activity, once exclusively legal, becomes routine, nonlawyer groups move in to take over the activity and perform its functions *better and cheaper*, eventually removing them from the area of legal practice. This progression may be seen in real property title opinions, handling of escrows, administration of trusts, processing of corporate filings, preparation of tax returns, and estate planning. Finally, an intangible factor in reduction of production costs may be the most consequential of all—a genuine desire throughout a law firm to lower the costs of legal services for each client whenever possible, thereby placing the firm's potential long-term gain ahead of short-term profit. As those firms that take the lead in putting their clients' financial interests ahead of their own are seen to prosper, change in the prevailing mores of all law firms will follow.

In this competitive race the large law firm with existing clients still retains the home-field advantage in any contest with would-be challengers. The firm already knows its clients' businesses, personnel, and methods of operation. Usually, cordial relations and mutual trust exist between lawyers and clients. Once a firm overcomes its initial abhorrence to price reductions, it can remain fully competitive as a low-cost producer of legal services for its clients.

COMPETITIVENESS: SALES COSTS

An equally important factor in reducing law firm costs is reduction of selling costs, that is, costs incurred in getting legal business. Formerly, the laws against champerty and maintenance proscribed direct solicitation and advertisement by lawyers, the only allowable form being formal announcements indicating a lawyer's specialty and past and present legal employments. Business came to a lawyer principally through reputation, but to acquire a reputation a lawyer needed business to work on, and for this he had to rely on referrals from other lawyers or on indirect advertising.

Referrals carried with them the strong disadvantage that the referring lawyer usually wanted (and got) a third of the total fees paid by the client. This payment, delicately described as a forwarding fee, was in fact a type of kickback of which the client ordinarily remained unaware, and whose effect was to increase the cost of legal services to the client by 50 percent. Bar associations, uncomfortable with the practice, generally took the position in their codes of ethics that such division of fees must be based on a division of work and responsibility, an ethic that did little more than provide a convenient fig leaf for unsavory prevailing practices. The lawyer who did not wish to enter the spongy ground of referral practice had to acquire business through indirect advertising, which meant appearances in circles where clients were likely to be found. Indirect advertising by a lawyer might include activities in clubs of all sorts, in chambers of commerce and civic associations, in charitable and cultural organizations, and in political and public affairs groups. The aim of these activities was to become favorably known to those who might someday need a lawyer. The process was comparable to a Spanish *paseo*, where at six in the evening the unmarried women promenade around the town square in their best clothes in hopes of attracting the attention of desirable suitors. As in the *paseo*, the potential client was supposed to make the first approach.

The promenade of indirect advertising consumed great quantities of time, and some lawyers, born salesmen, became a great deal better at it than others. A kind of legal specialty developed that can be called business promotion. When law firms were small, a firm's success was strongly affected by an individual lawyer's personal ability to attract business, and a lawyer able to generate a following could bring in sufficient business to occupy himself and other lawyers as well. The legal business promoter is a combination of two classic American types—the booster who creates the vision and the go-getter who closes the sale.[3] This ability to attract business was so prized that its possessors, now called rainmakers, were able to command a lion's share of fees for bringing business in the door, even when most or all actual legal work was performed by others. The consequence was that fees charged the client had to be large enough to compensate both the rainmaker and the lawyers who did the work. In effect, the rainmaker was paid an in-house forwarding fee, which became a selling cost comparable to payment of a commission by a seller of personal services (actor, entertainer, professional athlete) to an agent for locating a buyer for his services. Sales costs thus joined production costs and fixed overhead in determining total costs of delivery of legal services. Like many small businesses, these selling costs could be enormous, approximating the 33 percent paid for referrals. The story is told of Paul Cravath saying at a meeting to divide partnership profits, "I don't care how you divide it so long as I get my 50 percent."[4]

But times changed. In place of many thousands of relatively small law firms known only in limited circles, a lesser number of large law firms began to dominate the profession and to adopt institutional names, names of semi-mythical figures of past years long since absent from any active participation in the firm—Covington & Burling (Washington), Ropes & Gray (Boston), Sherman & Sterling (New York), O'Melveny & Myers (Los Angeles). These firms emphasized that all clients were clients of the firm and not of individual lawyers within the firm. In varying degrees they succeeded in establishing name identification as a provider of quality legal services, in effect building brand-name recognition in circles that might need their legal services. In similar fashion strong institutional links were established between important clients and their law firms—J. P. Morgan and Davis Polk; Goldman Sachs and Sullivan & Cromwell; Chevron Corporation and Pillsbury Madison—links that endured over generations independent of any one lawyer or client officer.

Paralleling this development, and in some respects at odds with it, has been a growing tendency of clients to pick and choose the lawyers within a firm they consider best-equipped to handle specific items of their legal business. Brand-name development focuses on the law firm as an assurance of quality. Specific-lawyer selection focuses on the abilities of the lawyer who is to do the work. The consequence of these twin developments, at least in a strong law firm, has been to strengthen the position of the firm as an institution, to strengthen the position of the lawyer who performs the legal services, and to weaken the once-dominant position of the rainmaker.

Paradoxically, as the importance of the rainmaker has declined in established large law firms, its role has increased in small law firms and in those large law firms that lack stability. Now that the large law firm has achieved brand-name recognition, the small firm needs the services of the booster and the go-getter more than ever; and the unstable large law firm that has not persuaded clients they are clients of the firm remains in dread of mass exodus of senior lawyers accompanied by their clients. As a consequence such firms may indulge the conduct of their rainmakers to an excessive degree, thereby heightening rather than reducing instability.

COMPETITIVENESS: ADVERTISING

After a long and lingering decline the laws against champerty and maintenance suffered a terminal blow in the 1977 Supreme Court ruling of *Bates v. Arizona*, holding that restrictions on lawyer advertising violate the constitutional right of free speech.[5] The floodgates of newspaper, magazine, telephone directory, radio, television, and direct mail advertising opened, as did direct solicitation of clients, cold calls by lawyers on those being sued, and advertisements by lawyers seeking clients with grievances against specific companies or products.[6] Bar associations, state courts, and state legislatures fought a losing battle against these new practices, their only successes until recently being the prohibition of false and misleading claims in lawyer advertising, a prohibition already applicable to business activities of all kinds. In the southern hemisphere of individual interests, personal injury litigation is routinely financed by lawyers and so aggressively solicited that residents of disaster areas sometimes debate which is worse, toxic leak or lawyer glut.[7] The sole recent regulatory success occurred in 1995 in Florida, where a rule postponing for 30 days direct written solicitation of calamity and accident victims was upheld in the Supreme Court by a 5-to-4 vote.[8]

The large law firm has not quite known how to take best advantage of its new freedom to advertise, fearing that projection of a cheap image would hurt rather than help its business. The best advertisement, of course, is a job well done, and the goal of any advertising is to make that fact known where it will do the most good. If under the new freedom to advertise and solicit business almost anything goes, the question remains: What works? Direct telephone solicitation has been tried by large law firms: "We would like to handle your sexual harassment cases," and

"We would like to represent you in your bankruptcy claim." With few exceptions such calls are counterproductive, in that the caller and his firm run the risk of being classified as common pests, comparable to the securities salesman who telephones at dinnertime with a sales pitch. Although direct solicitation by large law firms is rare, written communications from large law firms to existing and prospective clients have become common. Known as marketing letters, these report firm activities, new developments in given fields of law, along with some discreet solicitation: "If you have an overseas problem protecting your intellectual property (patents, copyrights, secret processes, logos, designs, etc.) our Mr. Z is an expert in the field and will be pleased to help you." Large law firms also publicize their expertise through direct advertising and through press releases to business and legal periodicals. Some firms sponsor radio and television broadcasts of programs likely to be watched by potential clients (symphony concerts, golf tournaments, news programs, business reports): "This program is sponsored by the law firm of Sheppard Mullin, a full-service law firm." The object of such advertising is to strengthen name recognition among an audience whose members employ law firms. Other firms, for example, Littler Mendelson (San Francisco), sponsor public seminars on the latest developments in their specialties, which naturally, feature as speakers lawyers of the sponsoring firms.[9] Still others operate speakers bureaus to fill from among their lawyers requests for speakers at business and community functions.

An important element of current law firm advertising consists of responses to invited solicitations. A retail chain opening stores in a new territory needs a law firm in the area to handle leasing and zoning problems, local taxation, personnel problems, and the like. It may interview several law firms for some or all of this work, in order to evaluate their abilities and their charges. Such events, known as beauty contests, involve competitive presentations and perhaps competitive bids. A law firm must be ready to make such presentations to existing or potential clients, and readiness requires continuing evaluation of law firm costs.

With this new freedom to advertise and solicit, large law firms have begun to employ public relations firms on retainer and to establish marketing and public relations sections of their own, whose task is to mesh the older indirect methods of publicizing a law firm's availability with the newer methods of direct solicitation and direct advertising. While it is difficult to predict the future extent of law firm advertising, present indications suggest the practices of the two hemispheres are beginning to converge.[10] In the southern hemisphere of individual interests, objectionable features of direct solicitation arc bcing reined in, and absolute freedom of speech is finding its limits, as it has in libel, obscenity, incitement to riot, and criminal conspiracy. In the northern hemisphere of collective interests, the rigors of competition are eroding gentlemanly inhibitions against public bragging and tooting one's own horn. Advertisements now include claims that range from generalizations (Davis Wright [Seattle], the first law firm to open an office in Shanghai, has the unique perspective and intimate knowledge necessary to break through the wall) to announcements of specific successes and quotations of testimonials (Patterson Belknap [New York] secured a defense verdict for a Johnson & Johnson subsidiary in a $45 million claim for patent infringement, "one of the major defense verdicts in 1994," reported the *National Law Journal*) to assertions of expertise in specific fields (Sidley & Austin [Chicago] has national presence, local expertise in the health care industry. To speak with one of our attorneys in Chicago, New York, Los Angeles, Washington, please call . . .).[11] Law firms now feel free to erect their own triumphal arches to publicize victorious campaigns.

It appears likely that future marketing by large law firms will concentrate on two fronts. The firm will accelerate its institutional advertising in a variety of ways, will not hesitate to publicize past and present successes, and will not shrink from claiming unique capabilities in specific areas. It will shun uninvited solicitations but remain fully prepared to respond with suitable proposals at the slightest suggestion. Additionally, the firm will require its specialist lawyers to intensify their personal activities in relevant business and legal circles in order to publicize their availability for specific legal employment and generate much of their own business. For lawyer specialists, these efforts can be highly focused and need not consume the inordinate amounts of time previously taken up by general, diffuse, indirect solicitation. For example, an intellectual property lawyer will play an active role in legal organizations and specialized bar groups that deal with intellectual property law, seek to appear before trade groups and legislative committees on issues relating to the subject, present papers on these issues at lawyer convocations, and publish articles in trade and legal periodicals on intellectual property developments. The goal of these activities is to become favorably known to officers and general counsel of business organizations active in the intellectual property field.

These changes portend a decline in selling costs of large law firms, the bulk of which has consisted of payment to rainmakers for bringing in business. With the growth of brand-name identification and of client selection of specific lawyers for specific tasks, the need for an expensive sales operation lessens, in much the same fashion that name recognition and an efficient distribution system for Ivory Soap lessened the need for drummers to visit country general stores to market the soap. Selling costs paid to a real estate agent for the sale of a house may be 6 percent, to a travel agent for the sale of an airplane ticket 8 percent, to an agent for marketing an actor's or athlete's personal services 10 to 15 percent. Selling costs of 33 percent for sales of legal services put the legal profession in the same category with such notoriously inefficient distribution systems as household furniture, hardware, and jewelry. Effective organization and effective advertising will lessen the need for the large law firm's equivalent of sales specialists to bring in business, lower the firm's selling costs, and enable it to market its services at competitive prices. If both production costs and selling costs are brought under control, a large law firm will have little difficulty achieving a position as a low-cost producer capable of competing with all comers.

JOB SATISFACTION

The challenge to a large law firm of providing job satisfaction for its lawyers tests to the utmost the skills of its management. Like other sizable business and professional organizations, the mega-firm faces the problem of making collaborative work within a large organization attractive to skilled professionals educated in a tradition of individual initiative. Pharmaceutical companies developing wonder drugs, electronic companies creating new marvels of communication and miniaturization, and aerospace companies providing transportation to the distant reaches of the solar system all employ highly skilled professionals to work in collaboration on large projects. The same is true in the more mundane spheres of tunnel and bridge design, machinery design, weather forecasting, and hospital operation. Each management must struggle with the problem of creating job satisfaction for skilled professionals who work in groups. Each seeks solutions that are compatible with its particular mission. While there are no perfect solutions, the more successful ones use variations of three elements: decentralization of the component parts of a project into separate working groups to the fullest extent consistent with retention of control over the project; encouragement of maximum individual initiative within a working group; full recognition of individual contributions whenever possible. (The engineer who designed the trigger mechanism for the second-stage booster of the rocket headed for Mars is honored in professional circles for the flawless performance of his design.)

As yet the average large law firm has not devoted a great amount of attention to the problem of job satisfaction but continues to rely on the potent motivation developed by the corporate law firm at the turn of the century—the premium paycheck—as the be-all and end-all of lawyer job satisfaction. But the paycheck is no longer enough. True job satisfaction for lawyers in today's large law firm requires major changes, some of which we now discuss.

Early Responsibility

Among changes long overdue is restoration to young lawyers of early professional responsibility. To find a solution for the frustration of juniors, we turn again to the early years of the corporate law firm. Many of these firms represented traction companies (streetcars and subways), whose corporate business was highly profitable. A handful of these firms, perhaps as an accommodation to their clients, also handled the routine litigation of the traction companies, involving a variety of damage claims for property loss and personal injuries arising from a company's day-to-day operations. Probably this work was only marginally profitable to the law firm, yet it possessed one valuable feature: It provided a diversity of cases that a beginning lawyer, after a relatively-short training period, could handle on his own, dealing directly with the client and with opposing counsel and assuming responsibility for the conduct of every phase of the case. Like a novice politician learning on the campaign trail how to handle hecklers, the beginning lawyer learned his craft by doing. Such work quickly matured the beginning lawyer, who as he acquired greater experience moved to more consequential cases. As a result, those law firms, among them Gibson Dunn (Los Angeles), possessed at all times a strong trial department with trial lawyers in all stages of development, competent to handle work on their own, from whom the most promising could be advanced to cases of major importance. Such firms followed the biblical injunction to make the man who has mastered little things ruler over many things.

To promote job satisfaction the large law firm must take the plunge and re-enter the arena of routine litigation, both to satisfy its juniors by giving them full opportunity to develop their talents, and to serve its own interests by building a staff of trial lawyers capable of handling cases at every level. If one or more of its top trial lawyers leaves, members of its strong replacement bench are readily available to take the field. A large law firm will have little difficulty getting all the routine litigation it needs, the only requisite being that it handle this business at competitive prices, which of course will be considerably less than its customary charges for major litigation. It is not necessary for the firm to enter all areas of routine individual controversy, although it should be fully competent to do so when the occasion demands. What it needs are representative lines of cases that will enable its junior lawyers to acquire the skills needed to advance their professional development, including the skill of keeping the cost of litigation in balance with the stakes involved.

Similar considerations apply to office lawyers who handle the legal aspects of business deals or who translate clients' wishes into valid legal instruments. Again, early assumption of full responsibility for meaningful work matures talents and improves job satisfaction. While no businessman is likely to entrust a $100 million negotiation to a lawyer of two years' experience, many will do so in a $25,000 deal, particularly when the junior lawyer is affiliated with a large law firm. As in trial work, the large law firm in past years has generally shunned small business matters as only marginally profitable and overlooked their usefulness as training. If a large law firm operates a small or start-up business department, charging competitive prices for its services, its younger business lawyers will acquire an opportunity to exercise responsibility and develop the skills needed to deal with clients, to negotiate with opposing lawyers, and to achieve workable outcomes. Likewise, the law firm is furthering its own interests by grooming understudies capable of replacing its business stars, when and as needed. While small and start-up business activity within a law firm need not always remain marginal, as the success of high-technology start-up clients in Silicon Valley has demonstrated, the possibility of bonanza growth remains incidental to the main benefit to the law firm of increased job satisfaction among its younger lawyers through early exercise of responsibility.

In effect, the large law firm will be running its own postgraduate training programs with curriculums based on learning by doing. These programs will also address the problem of anonymity and lack of recognition of the junior lawyer who works in a large law firm. Direct access to clients will bring client recognition of a job well done. Appearances in court or in negotiations with other lawyers will bring a degree of professional recognition of lawyerly talents, albeit within limited circles. Nonetheless, even modest professional recognition is vastly preferable to the anonymity of a junior lawyer in a large office, known professionally only to superiors and fellow workers.

Law firm entry at competitive prices into routine legal business provides a further indicator of a relative decline in salaries for beginning lawyers in large law firms, who more and more are coming to be seen as interns. Here we find a paradox. How can lower earnings improve job satisfaction? If earnings were the sole factor in job satisfaction, obviously they would not. But the decisive factor at the beginning of a professional career is not money but professional development that leads to full stature as a lawyer. Acceptance of lower salaries tells the familiar story of benefits deferred to secure future benefits of greater size—the same motivation that induces high school graduates to relinquish the immediate earnings of a job in favor of a college education and that induces law school graduates to accept judicial clerkships at lesser pay. For a junior lawyer the choice in favor of professional development is usually easy to make.

Diversification of Experience

A second major cause of job dissatisfaction in large law firms, less immediate than lack of early responsibility but of increasing importance over the years, arises from the narrowness of a lawyer's experience as a consequence of specialization. The beginning lawyer in a large law firm is usually bright, articulate, skilled in book learning, and has associated with persons of similar abilities most of her adult life. The large law firm provides a continuation of the same kind of association. The catholic experience of the lawyer of earlier generations who dealt with all kinds of people and problems and knew the flow of events over several generations has gone. Instead of a diversity of experience in law, a discipline described by Holmes as a seamless web, the junior lawyer finds herself immersed in a small segment of law in exclusive association with others like her. Realization of this narrowness, together with the prospect of even greater narrowness in the years ahead, brings a sense of uneasiness, of values askew, of anomie. A law firm must do what it can to meliorate this narrowness by encouraging its juniors to acquire some breadth of professional experience. Although a modicum of diversity can be acquired within the confines of the firm, more is needed. Such diversity lies at hand in the form of public legal employment, which the law firm should encourage through sabbaticals, leaves of absence, detached service, and the like. In so doing it is again serving its own long-term interest in improving its lawyers' skills and abilities and in developing future firm leadership.

In past years law firms did not encourage public service by juniors at lower and intermediate levels of government. Most law firm policies emphasized the primacy of billable hours and profit augmentation through leverage. Departures from practices designed to maximize these items were viewed with disfavor. Junior lawyers knew as well as anyone else that in the quest for the brass ring of promotion to senior (ownership) status, their hourly billings and current profitability remained the primary coinage. Other activities were usually viewed by law firms and juniors alike as side excursions that could cause a junior to lag her contemporaries and penalize her career. This viewpoint sometimes became obsessive, as in the instance of the lawyer in contention for promotion to senior status who refused to take more than two weeks' leave for the birth of her child for fear she would fall behind her competitors in the race. As long as law firms and their lawyers alike treated other employments as distractions from the main chance, diversity of experience languished. In its own interest the large law firm must do what it can to facilitate freedom of movement for its lawyers between the firm and public law offices in order to give its juniors an opportunity to acquire outside legal experience without penalizing their firm prospects. A tour of duty in a government law office exposes a junior to quite different interests from those usually represented by a private firm and can be a stringent corrective to any narrowness that arises from experience solely in a large law firm. And for the same reasons the law firm likewise will benefit from policies that encourage its seniors to undertake tours of public duty as members of commissions, advisers to legislative committees, or special investigators in extended state or federal inquiries. In its own interest a law firm should foster such comings and goings to help its juniors and lower-tier seniors become abler lawyers and develop the skills of a generalist. Once the value to the firm of these forays has been recognized, the mechanics of their application will present no greater difficulties than they do in university employment.

Contract Tenure

Lawyer discontent in large law firms is exacerbated by the continued use of a law firm structure that has become obsolete, one based on a master–servant relationship that divides lawyers into two groups: the lawyer owners, called partners, and the lawyer employees, called associates. An organizational structure that suited a firm of 20 or 30 lawyers continues to be used by today's mega-firms. The partnership grouping implies that partners own and run the firm and will continue to function as partners indefinitely, that associates serve as employees at will, subject to termination at the pleasure of the partners. The origin of this system of master and servant derives from the medieval guild relationship of master and apprentice, under which an apprentice paid a fee to work under a master without compensation for a period of years until he had learned the trade and could become a journeyman, after which he could go into business with his former master or operate by himself as master and in turn accept apprentices to work for him. During the late nineteenth century, most legal training was obtained in law offices, and full-time law schools played a subordinate role in legal education. Under the then-prevailing legal-apprentice system, the apprentice worked for his master until he had learned the law, and only then could he set up in practice for himself. At the turn of the century law firms still functioned under this system. For example, Henry L. Stimson entered Elihu Root's office in 1891 and became a partner in 1893.[12] The real significance of his change in status was that he had completed his apprenticeship and become fully capable of functioning as a lawyer.

When the corporate law firm came into being, it modified the apprentice system by paying a living wage to beginning lawyers to work under the supervision of a senior lawyer, and, as corporate law matters grew increasingly complicated, by using multiple juniors as assistants to a senior, juniors who continued in that status for periods of up to seven or eight years, at which time only a fraction of them became partners while the rest moved or had moved elsewhere. The new partners became part of management and were implicitly assured of tenure, that is, a permanent position with the firm. As long as law firms remained small, the system could work. Partners as a collegial body made all major decisions. A genuine difference in function existed between those running the firm and its lawyer employees. But as law firms exploded in size to number 200, 400, 600, or more lawyers, and a firm of 600 lawyers was often composed of 200 partners and 400 associates, the difference in function between the two groups attenuated. A small group of perhaps 30 partners controlled the firm and ran its operations, while the remaining 170 partners lacked any real management function. The latter's principal differentiation from associates was some say in the selection of management and possession of an implied tenure that precluded termination except for misbehavior. But as events of the last few years have demonstrated, differences between nonmanagement partners and associates are minimal. The partner has a monthly drawing account and a share of net profits at the end of the year. The associate has a monthly salary and a bonus at the end of the year. Both can be fired. On termination a partner receives whatever share he has of partnership capital (tangible assets, accounts receivable, work in progress). An associate receives termination pay. The substantive difference between partner and associate is about the same as the difference between an employee who owns stock in the corporation for which he works and an employee who does not. Yet in law firms the rigid difference in status, inherited from an earlier epoch, continues in form even though its substance has vanished, continues at a time when partners at firm meetings use name tags to identify one another. Under this antiquated structure job discontent has become endemic within both groups. Associates may feel they are like squeezed oranges, to be thrown away after their juice has been extracted. The nonmanagement partner may feel apprehensive about the reality of his status and consequently may not hesitate to move elsewhere when opportunity beckons. The rigidity of a system derived from the historic master–apprentice relationship has become increasingly counterproductive, and law firms are beginning to experiment with new classification systems. For example, Davis Polk (New York) has six categories of lawyers (senior counsel, retired partner, member of the firm, counsel, senior attorney, and associate), and Paul Weiss (New York) has five.[13] These new classifications may be little more helpful than those of the banks that once had hundreds of first, second, and third vice presidents, but they do suggest that law firms are in the beginning stages of a shift from a regime of status to one of contract, from a triangular structure to one of hexagonal shape.

A regime of contract, with specified compensation for all lawyers in dollar amounts and/or share of net profits, with specified terms of em-ployment (one year, two years, three years, five years) and with speci-fication of voting or nonvoting rights in the selection of management, might bring greater stability to large law firm operations than now exists under a fictitious tenure for seniors and uncertainty of prospect for jun-iors. Individual employment contracts are now common in the business world for senior management and for highly skilled professionals. Would the large law firm similarly benefit by adoption of a contract system under a grouping of senior management and contract professionals? Would stability and job satisfaction increase? Whatever the answers to these questions may be, it is clear that change in law firm structure lies ahead.

18

L'Envoi—Visions in the Crystal Ball

In earlier chapters we have seen the development of the large law firm into a powerful instrument possessing extraordinary capabilities but also containing serious flaws. To diagnose the large law firm's flaws is easier than to devise solutions, and to devise solutions is easier than to put them into effect. Does the large law firm as currently constituted possess the capacity to mend its flaws, adjust to new, rapidly-evolving conditions, and face down new competitors, or will it give way to more responsive institutions that do a better job?

LAWYER CONTROL OVER LEGAL SERVICES

The distinctive feature of private law firm practice has been exclusive ownership of law firms by lawyers—non-lawyers and outside groups being legally prohibited from ownership and control.[1] Such is not an inevitable concomitant of licensed professional activity, as may be seen in engineering, contracting, educational, and medical-care organizations. It is entirely possible that future legal services will be delivered through lay organizations or publicly-held corporations that contract to perform legal services and employ licensed lawyers to do the work, much as Vidal Sassoon operates or franchises a worldwide chain of beauty salons that employ locally-licensed beauticians and hairdressers to do the professional work. In the legal world tentative steps in this direction may be seen in moves by business enterprises to purchase for cash direct financial interests in pending speculative lawsuits.[2] Another move in the same direction is issuance by corporations of participating certificates in the expected proceeds of pending lawsuits, such as the Contingent Litigation Recovery Participation Interests issued by California Federal Bank in its $425 million suit against the federal government, certificates that traded on the Nasdaq National Market at prices ranging from $4 to $7 3/8, until a favorable Supreme Court ruling in a related case jumped the price to $11 15/16.[3] The next step in such an evolution could be permanent publicly-owned investment organizations to syndicate directly to the general public packages of speculative lawsuits, much as venture capital groups have arisen to finance speculative business projects. Almost inevitably, those raising the money would call the tune and run the show. From speculative lawsuit ventures to contracts by non-lawyer groups to provide legal services is not too distant a step. Indeed, it is already here on a modest basis in the form of insurance contracts for consultative and referral legal services[4] and in the form of contracts by non-lawyer groups to deliver to corporate buyers at fixed prices legal research reports on any specified subject, with the reports prepared by specialist lawyers hired by the non-lawyer group for each project.[5] Some railroad companies and insurers have captive law firms in their own buildings at their beck and call. We know little of the financial details of these arrangements, but we can infer that such law firms are wholly responsive to the wishes of their landlord and dominant client. If non-lawyer organizations are seen to do a better job in providing quality legal services at lesser cost, a legal order could develop under which most major legal services would be delivered by subsidiaries of publicly-held corporations, and the large lawyer-owned firm will have gone the way of the steam locomotive and the open-hearth furnace.

History is littered with wrecked institutions that clung too long without change to the successes that created them—eighteenth-century salons, nineteenth-century lyceum lecture circuits, twentieth-century motion-picture palaces. In the legal area a conspicuous example of institutional failure to adjust is the English Inns of Court, semiautonomous institutions that arose in the fourteenth century for the training and selection of lawyers and judges and that had become so dominant by Elizabethan times that to find an equivalent today one would need to combine a top law school, a strong bar association, a leading law firm, and a French *grande école* to produce the teachers, lawyers, judges, and top government officials turned out by the Inns. In their heyday Inns even became leading patrons of the musical and theatrical arts, sponsoring the first known performances of Shakespeare's *Twelfth Night* and *The Comedy of Errors.*[6] Yet by the middle of the seventeenth century these organizations had dwindled to irrelevancy, not to be revived until the nineteenth century and then only in attenuated form. The factor that made the Inns of Court obsolete was the growing use in legal studies of printed law reports and legal treatises, which began to replace the oral moots, exercises, and memorizations that had constituted the heart of the Inns' activities. Students resorted to books as a faster and cheaper method of learning law. Lawyers and judges found Inn participation no longer essential for professional advancement. Monarchs acquired their top ministers elsewhere. The invention of printing had toppled yet another medieval institution.[7]

There is some resemblance between the spread of printing as a challenge to medieval ways and the spread of data storage and retrieval as a challenge to business as usual in the legal profession. Dramatic changes in the speed and cost of data processing occur each year, and computers have begun to monopolize the tasks of locating and abstracting documents, indexing and cross-referencing their contents, compiling digests of law on any subject, and providing access to documentary models adaptable for current use—work heretofore performed at greater expense by or under the immediate supervision of lawyers. Like the displacement of hand-entry bookkeeping by machine-entry accounting, these developments will bring dramatic changes in twenty-first-century delivery of legal services. The trend toward greater amalgamation and concentration of legal-service providers is likely to continue, along with further decline in individual and small-firm practice. In this centralization the great unresolved issue is whether legal services will continue to be delivered by law firms as we now know them or by publicly- and privately-owned business organizations. A related question is whether changed conditions will encourage major consumers of legal services to do more of their own legal work, either by continuing to expand their own legal departments or by making greater use of the non-lawyer consultants who vie with lawyers in overlapping areas of expertise.

Present-day vulnerabilities of the large law firm converge on its weaknesses in management, reflected most publicly and conspicuously by a perceived inability to maintain order in its own ranks and to deliver cost-effective services. Inevitably, if law firms owned and operated by lawyers cannot run their businesses efficiently, other organizations will arise that can, as is happening to physician-dominated groups in the health-care field. It is within the realm of possibility that large law firms of the future will operate as divisions of conglomerates, as do today many stockbrokers, investment bankers, and publishers. Those who do the legal work will remain the same, but direction and control of the law firm itself will pass into the hands of those who are skilled in management, production, and marketing. A precursor of such a development may be seen in the activities of American accounting firms in Europe, where Arthur Andersen operates a law firm of 240 lawyers in Paris and is also reported to be the fastest-growing law firm in Britain, and where Price Waterhouse operates out of Brussels a network of European law offices employing 250 lawyers.[8]

These possibilities remain, in the author's view, no more than possibilities. First, competition among large law firms and client demands for change are powerful correctors of abuses, and law firms under these pressures are recognizing the need for change. Their more astute leaders already seek to assert greater control over firm operations in order to eliminate conditions that make shoddy practices and excessive charges possible. They are also aware of the dangers of allowing new and formidable competition to gain a foothold. The tangible threat of displacement by more efficient lay organizations, together with a vision of the large law firm as an enduring institution—a cathedral of responsibility and integrity within a troubled profession—have focused the attention of these leaders on the twin necessities of strong firm culture and strong positive economics. As these leaders realign their operations to achieve these objectives, other large law firms will follow, and those that do not risk extinction. Changes in law firm operations can be made relatively quickly, in that law firms are not dependent on absentee owners, large capital investment, long-term contracts, or collective bargaining agreements. Given the number of talented persons within these firms we can expect many, perhaps a majority, to respond effectively to the new conditions and survive with increased strength.

A second reason for large law firm survival is that we have experienced 20 years under a regime of minimum lawyer accountability, with results that have proved highly unsatisfactory to the general public and clients alike. The old regime had many imperfections but its limited controls moderated to some degree the occupational excesses to which lawyers are prone. Those earlier controls included qualitative and quantitative limitations on bar admissions, prohibitions against advertising and direct solicitation, and limited lawyer mobility from home base. But the tidal wave of change that shattered the sea wall of lawyers' traditional manners and customs swept away existing restraints against excesses before substitute barriers could be built. Their disappearance left the profession largely destitute of effective controls over lawyer conduct. Some commentators have viewed the dissolution of these earlier controls as a tragedy (Glendon, Kronman).[9] Others have welcomed their disappearance as the opening of a window in the guild cartel that now admits the fresh air of competition (Posner, Abel).[10] But whether in the abstract one views the old regime as a distillation of the sweetness of life or sees it as a blight on economic enterprise of which we are well rid, 20-years' concrete experience under the new dispensation has given us a vivid appreciation of what we have lost. There is little inclination to dilute professional accountability further by turning legal organizations over to lay control. On the contrary, the prevailing current flows strongly in the direction of new controls to replace the old ones whose benefits we had taken for granted. All signs indicate that the general public strongly favors reinstatement of professional responsibility and increased authority for the instruments of professional control, many of which are in the process of being restructured to include a strong, sometimes controlling, element of lay input. For example, 6 of the 23 governors of the California State Bar must be lay persons, as must 6 of the 11 members of California's Commission on Judicial Performance.[11] As much as anything else, this strong public sentiment in favor of professional accountability will shield law firms from conglomerate or lay control.

LAWYERS AS BUSINESSMEN

What specific changes in law firm activities can we expect? By way of counteroffensive against lay competition, some law firms have sought to become conglomerates themselves, either directly or through subsidiaries, by invading such nonlegal areas of enterprise as business promotion and finance, lobbying and public relations, management consulting, and publishing.[12] Examples include Arnold & Porter (Washington), which in 1989 operated three subsidiaries to provide consulting services, one for banks, one for real estate development, and one for lobbying and crisis management (i.e., public relations),[13] and Riordan & McKinzie (Los Angeles) which operates a venture capital subsidiary under the name Riordan, Lewis & Haden. Perhaps the most active of these areas is business promotion and finance. A promotional lawyer no longer merely advises a client what steps he may legally take and then prepares documents to carry out his client's objectives, but becomes a business organizer, finder of funds, broker of business opportunities, and launcher of new enterprises, activities once considered the exclusive province of the businessman. For some lawyers the lure of these areas is irresistible. They argue that they are experts on legal form (which they are), that form is substance made manifest (which it is), and therefore they are experts on substance and should be compensated accordingly. The conclusion does not follow. By and large, lawyers are not particularly well suited for promotional business activities. Businessmen are risk-takers, lawyers risk-avoiders. Businessmen look to the future, lawyers to the past. Businessmen are creators, lawyers the conservators of the creations of others. By training and temperament most lawyers are not cut out for the entrepreneurial life.

Beyond this generic incompatibility lies a dark side to the shimmering vision of easy riches through business promotion. As long as a law firm merely gives legal advice, does not participate as a principal in a transaction, and limits its fees to amounts that may be justified for legal services, it remains relatively safe from the danger of liability for a failed promotion. But when it has acted and been paid as a principal in a promotion that has gone sour, those who have lost money—investors, lenders of money, sellers of businesses—do not hesitate to include the law firm in their list of defendants from whom they seek to recoup losses. Similarly, when lawyers engage in extensive public relations campaigns on behalf of their clients, they become vulnerable to lawsuits that name them, along with their clients, as co-conspirators in fraud, as is happening to law firms active in research projects to exonerate tobacco companies from liability to smokers.[14] Lawyers are discovering that when they enter deals as active participants and apparent principals, they have given hostages to fortune. Some firms have sought to minimize potential liability by creating separate legal entities to carry on the nonlegal aspects of their activities, but it is a safe bet that attempts to insulate a parent law firm from liability for the misconduct of an affiliate will enjoy no greater degree of success than businesses themselves have experienced in their attempts to avoid liability for questionable acts of a subsidiary. The downside risks of most nonlegal activities are so apparent that any general entry of law firms into deal-making, financing, and business management appears unlikely.

An additional consideration against lawyer participation as principals in business ventures or business management is that such participation may compromise the lawyer's most valuable contribution to his client—his ability to give disinterested and at times unwelcome advice, to view matters from a different perspective than that of the participants, and to provide advice unclouded by the prospect of personal gain or loss. Firms such as Cravath Swaine have always prohibited their lawyers from investing in, or serving as directors of, their clients.[15] While this conception of a lawyer's proper sphere has always been a minority view (that of the vast majority being that service as a director is valuable to the client in giving the law firm a better understanding of the client's operations and in cementing relations with the client), recent explosive growth in promoters' and directors' liability is causing second thoughts.[16] Are we lawyers or are we businessmen? To a greater or lesser degree lawyers are beginning to recognize that two different and sometimes contradictory functions are involved, that there are genuine losses when the two are mixed. The strong probability is that lawyers will continue to concentrate on what they do best: guiding the flood waters of new developments, new demands, new discoveries, new relationships between groups and among individuals, into existing flood plains and storage reservoirs so as to adapt an existing system to new conditions. There is a plentiful supply of this work, and competent lawyers have little need to seek out activities for which they are ill-equipped.

FUTURE LAW FIRM STRUCTURE

What sort of law firm will survive and prosper? One vision of the future sees the law firm as a mere service organization providing equipment, facilities, support services, and central staff for individual lawyers and for disparate clusters of lawyers having little in common with one another, minimally sharing profits and losses, operating under provisional arrangements subject to constant renegotiation in which current profits are the sole bargaining chips, and engaging in an endless ronde of lateral arrivals and departures. Every superior is seen as a barrier to be pushed aside, every subordinate or new arrival as a potential rival to be cut down to size. This Hobbesian view of tooth-and-claw association, expressed in lawyer-speak as "you eat what you kill," guarantees continuing instability by its implicit rejection of teamwork and collaborative effort to achieve integrity and quality control (the strength of the pack) in favor of a regime of internal and external cutthroat competition. The law firm becomes little more than a booking and billing office that sends vaudeville acts on tour but neither possesses authority nor exercises responsibility over their performance. Any entity that expects to endure as an organization must generate reciprocal loyalty between individual and organization. The chilling accounts of law firms that have moved toward an ethos of short-term individual survival are reminiscent of Hollywood in its bonanza days, when the only serious information ever sought from an actor, director, or producer was the gross of his latest picture. The so-called cold reality of the 1990s represents no more than a transitory phenomenon, a superficial response to intensified competition that abandons the genuine benefits of collegiality, of collaborative association, of loyalty up and loyalty down, in favor of a regime of each for himself. Such atomistic arrangements have no long-term future.

LAW FIRM SIZE

What of the future size of law firms? From time to time there is speculation that the 600-lawyer firms will put the 200-lawyer firms out of business by a process of merger and consolidation similar to that which has produced six national accounting firms that dominate that profession. Accounting, however, is not an adversarial activity. Within a given trade or industry, an accounting firm, like an architectural or engineering firm, may easily work for a number of competitors. Matters are quite different in the legal world, where representation by a single law firm of more than one major competitor in a given industry is rare, in that companies aggressively competing against one another feel uncomfortable sharing the same law firm. Additionally, major controversies, such as oil spills, bankruptcies, and product-liability claims, involve a myriad of different interests for whose resolution scores of different law firms may be needed to represent interests that conflict. Any law firm failure to deal fully with possible conflicting interests may return at a later time to haunt the firm, expose it to heavy damages, and darken its reputation for competency. For these reasons, although large law firms will continue their steady growth in size, their consolidation into a handful of national firms is most improbable.

Other speculation on the future size of large law firms centers on whether with the continued increase in legal specialties a firm or branch office of 50 lawyers can continue to maintain a credible presence as a full-service law office. The minimum number of lawyers needed to operate a law office covering major problems of collective organizations may well increase to 100 or 200 lawyers. This possibility directly affects the future course of large law firms with multiple branch offices, for at present only a minority of these branches contains the minimum number of lawyers now needed to claim full-service capability. While small size poses no difficulty for branches in suburban areas close to a major office of the firm, when the specialist whose services are needed is 500 or 1,500 miles away, a client with an urgent problem may not be satisfied with telecommunication or with the delayed arrival in person of the specialist, whose travel expenses the client knows that one way or another he will pay.

Current deployment of personnel among the branches of large law firms suggests that several different approaches are being taken. Some firms focus on a central office with small branches to provide services mainly for clients of the central office, the pattern of leading New York firms. Others limit branches to offices of sufficient size to possess the potential for independent full-service operations, the pattern of leading Chicago and Los Angeles firms. Over time it is possible that such branches, like the colonies sent out by the ancient Greeks and by modern state universities with multiple campuses, may equal or surpass in size and prestige that of the home office. This may be already happening with the Philadelphia firm of Morgan Lewis, whose New York and Washington offices equal the size of the home office.[17] Another large group of firms shows no discernible pattern of staffing but operates branches both large and small, including Chicago's Baker & McKenzie (55 offices), Cleveland's Jones Day (20 offices), and New York's Skadden Arps (21 offices). The future development of branch offices remains cloudy, but the continuing emergence of new specialties, the growing complexity of old ones, and the need to put branch offices on a firm financial footing all suggest further growth in the size of branches, a growth that may stimulate more law firm mergers and more lateral movement of groups of lawyers. It is possible to envisage floating law firms that, like international banks such as the Hongkong and Shanghai Banking Corporation, geographically reposition themselves and their personnel wherever the action is most promising.[18] It may be noted that prestigious medical institutions are also colonizing geographically-distant areas, such as the Mayo Clinic of Rochester, Minnesota, with flourishing branches in Scottsdale, Arizona, and Jacksonville, Florida.[19]

TIME FUTURE

The effect of intensified competition among large law firms will be severely felt by small law firms engaged in collective law and by lawyers practicing in areas of individual law. As discussed earlier, the small law firm specializing in one or more aspects of collective law has survived because of its lower fees and willingness to handle less desirable business. But in an era of intensified competition the price differential that kept it in operation will narrow. A further handicap of the small law firm is the growing need in law firms of all sizes for increased amounts of capital in order to provide more attractive credit terms to clients, to accept long-deferred fee matters, and to absorb the risks of major engagements gone awry. The strong sentiment against lay ownership of law firms inhibits solicitation of outside equity capital. In the resultant internal financing of law firm operations the advantage is with the large law firm, which possesses superior borrowing capability and superior ability to spread the risks of unanticipated losses among multiple engagements, following the carnival principle that what you lose on the coconuts you make on the shies. There will be exceptions to the general decline of small law firms, brought about by the charisma of a particular lawyer, the closeness of his relationship with a specific client or industry, his skill and effectiveness in a specialized field, or his celebrity status in a high-profile activity (white-collar crime, hostile takeovers, airplane crashes). Even here, in major undertakings the small law firm often needs the assistance of a large law firm to provide the resources and staff to carry the project to completion, as happened in the billion-dollar Pennzoil-Texaco litigation, in which Joseph Jamail's firm (seven lawyers) needed the collaboration of Baker & Botts (Houston, 410 lawyers) for the prosecution of the case.[20] The exceptions of small law firm prosperity will not ordinarily survive the departure of the persons who kept the firm viable.

Intensified competition among law firms large and small will heighten the relentless pressure of the past few years on lawyers engaged in representing individual and not collective interests. Small craft advisories are flying in every port. On one side the continuing centralization of collective interests is removing more and more legal business from the sphere of individual vindication. On the other the large law firm and its little sister, the boutique, continue to invade the most profitable areas of individual-interest practice, armed with the potential to provide faster and better service. These twin developments portend a bleak future for the group that in a simpler day constituted the dominant element within the profession. To an increasing degree its members will be forced into public legal employment, corporate law departments, large law firms, or into other occupations. The law school diploma and the steel engraving of Abraham Lincoln on the wall no longer suffice.

To conclude that large law firms are the probable legal vehicles of the future is not to conclude that all large law firms are equal. Some are a great deal more equal than others, and for a revolving group of perhaps two dozen firms throughout the country prestige will remain a marketable factor for which the sun of supply and demand stands still. The remaining 800 firms and branches will compete fiercely to maintain or improve position, and perhaps even secure elevation to the ranks of the magic two dozen. Clients will enjoy the full benefit of this continuing competition.

Once the large law firm gets its house in order by adjusting its operations to today's competitive markets, by creating working conditions for its lawyers that reconcile collaborative efforts with professional recognition and collegiality, and by putting the importance of money into proper perspective, the bulk of the legal profession will follow suit. Those elements of the profession that do not will risk extinction. Once lawyers have adjusted their conduct and expectations to today's conditions, public distrust of the profession will die down, and lawyers will again hold their heads high as members of a profession in which they take pride.

Notes

PREFACE

1. Derek Bok, *The Cost of Talent* (New York, The Free Press, 1993); Sol M. Linowitz, *The Betrayed Profession* (New York, Charles Scribner's Sons, 1994); Anthony T. Kronman, *The Lost Lawyer* (Cambridge, Mass., Harvard University Press, 1993); Mary Ann Glendon, *A Nation Under Lawyers* (New York, Farrar Straus, 1994); Richard A. Posner, *Overcoming Law* (Cambridge, Mass., Harvard University Press, 1995).

CHAPTER 1. THE PARADOX

1. U.S. Dept of Commerce, *U.S. Industrial Outlook 1994*, 9–1, 40–2, 43–2, 51–3. A later, more accurate figure published in December 1994 by the Census Bureau, U.S. Dept of Commerce, reports gross revenues for legal services in 1992 as $101 billion, *1992 Census of Service Industries*, pp. 12, 21, 53. The earlier figure of $97 billion has been used here to keep revenue reporting for legal services consistent with figures reported for other industries.

2. "The Am Law 100," *The American Lawyer* (July–Aug. 1995).

3. "The NLJ 250," *The National Law Journal* (Oct. 9, 1995).

4. *The Lawyer's Almanac 1996* (Englewood Cliffs, N.J., Aspen Law & Business, 1996). In 1994 the 700 largest firms of 51 lawyers or more totaled 102,000 lawyers.

5. This and other economic discussion of the legal profession draws heavily

on R. Sander and E. Williams, "Why Are There So Many Lawyers?" 14 *Law and Social Inquiry* 431 (1989); M. Galanter and T. Palay, *The Tournament of Lawyers* (Chicago, University of Chicago Press, 1991); and J. Heinz and E. Laumann, *Chicago Lawyers, The Social Structure of the Bar* (New York, Russell Sage Foundation, 1982). For legal services as a percentage of national income, see Sander and Williams, Table 2, p. 435, who report a percentage of 0.47 in 1950 and of 1.38 in 1987. The number of lawyers and their ratio in the general population, as calculated by Sander and Williams (Table 1, p. 433), are:

Year	Lawyers and Judges	U.S. Population	Lawyers Per Million
1950	184,000	151 million	1200
1988	757,000	244 million	3100
	To update with current estimates:		
1994	864,000	260 million	3100

(1994 lawyer population from *The Wall Street Journal*, Jan. 13, 1995. U.S. population for 1994 from *Statistical Abstract of the United States, 1994*. The *1994 Abstract* reports the number of lawyers in 1991 as 805,000.)

CHAPTER 2. INVENTION OF THE CORPORATE LAW FIRM AND ITS EVOLUTION INTO THE LARGE LAW FIRM

1. For Cravath Swaine, see R. Swaine, *The Cravath Firm* Vol. 1, pp. 669, 774 (New York, Ad Press, 1946). For Sullivan & Cromwell, see N. Lisagor and F. Lipsius, *A Law Unto Itself* 32 (New York, William Morrow, 1988).

2. A comprehensive history of law firms from 1900 to 1960 appears in M. Galanter and T. Palay, *The Tournament of Lawyers* Chaps. 2, 3 (Chicago, University of Chicago Press, 1991).

3. This and other examples assume a fictitious constant dollar and ignore the tenfold price inflation of the past 60 years reflected in the Consumer Price Index. During this period the relationship between corporate law firm charges and general practitioner charges remained roughly the same, regardless of charges in the price level. Thus at one time charges for incorporation might be $50 by the corporate law firm and $100 by the general practitioner, at another $500 by the corporate law firm and $1,000 by the general practitioner.

CHAPTER 3. EMERGENCE OF THE LARGE LAW FIRM AS THE DOMINANT ELEMENT OF THE PROFESSION

1. ABA Membership Dues Schedule for 1996 lists thirty-two sections, divisions, and forums.

2. *The Lawyer's Almanac 1996* (Englewood Cliffs, N.J., Aspen Law & Business, 1995).

3. 1937 statistics are from *Martindale-Hubbell Law Directory, 1937*. (New York and San Francisco firms in 1937 listed partners only.) 1995 statistics are from "The NLJ 250," *The National Law Journal* (Oct. 9, 1995).

4. The percentage groupings are best estimates. U.S. Census figures report

legal service providers and their employees together and do not provide figures for lawyers only. Government estimates of lawyers and their legal categories, such as those of the U.S. Dept. of Commerce in its annual publication *Statistical Abstract of the United States*, are generally based on reports from bar associations and from legal directories like *Martindale-Hubbell Law Directory*, which are subject to defects of double-counting (lawyers active in several states), of inaccurate classification, and of omissions (inactive and nonreporting lawyers). See R. Sander and E. Williams, "Why Are There So Many Lawyers?" 14 *Law and Social Inquiry*, 431, 433–42 (1989). As an example of the inadequacy of statistics about lawyers, the State Bar of California, membership in which is compulsory for all California lawyers, reported in October 1995 a total membership of 147,000, of which 29,000 were inactive, a proportion of almost 20 percent; see *California Bar Journal* (November 1995). The Department of Commerce's *Statistical Abstract of the U.S. 1994*, Table 327, relying on information from *Martindale-Hubbell Law Directory*, reported the number of lawyers in the United States in 1991 as 805,000, of which 37,000 were classified as inactive or retired, a proportion less than 5 percent. This difference between 5 percent and 20 percent illustrates the lack of precise information on active lawyer participation and affiliation and the need to rely on estimates.

Sander and Williams, *supra* at 442, estimated the proportion of lawyers in active private practice in 1980 as 68 percent, a percentage that has continued to decline with the growth in government legal employment, corporate legal employment, and miscellaneous and inactive status. This figure parallels that of the Chicago law survey of J. Heinz and E. Laumann, *Chicago Lawyers, The Social Structure of the Bar* (New York, Russell Sage Foundation, 1982), which found that 51 percent of all lawyers were in solo or small firms (under 30 lawyers) and 16 percent were in large law firms (p. 13) for a total of 67 percent. The author estimates the proportion in 1994 of all lawyers in active private practice as 60 percent, of which a quarter practiced in large law firms. Other indication that a quarter of lawyers in private practice are in firms of 50 lawyers or more is found in *"Law Office Management and Administration Report,"* September 1994, p. 16, reporting that new lawyer employment by law firms of 50 or more lawyers was 26 percent of the total of new lawyers in private practice.

A comparable report by the Institute of Civil Justice at RAND, in its 1994 survey of California lawyers made for the California State Bar, shows lawyer employment in organizations of 51 or more lawyers as 24 percent of lawyers in private practice; *California Bar Journal*, San Francisco, November 1994.

5. J. Heinz and E. Laumann, *Chicago Lawyers: The Social Structure of the Bar* Chap. 10 (New York, Russell Sage Foundation, 1982).

6. Sander and Williams, *supra* note 2, show in Table 5, p. 441, the sources of law firms' receipts in percentages:

Year	Individual	Business	Govt./Other
1967	55	39	6
1982	44.5	48.6	6.9

7. S. Linowitz, *The Betrayed Profession* 89, 199 (New York, Scribner's, 1994).

8. Sander and Williams, *supra* note 2, at 439, 440, concluded in 1989 that

"the relative receipts of the big firms have grown faster than the relative size of their staffs," from which they infer that these firms "have become significantly more affluent (on a per-lawyer basis) relative to the rest of the legal community."

9. The Consumer Price Index for Urban Consumers, kept since 1913 by the U.S. Department of Labor, provides our most reliable index of the measure of inflation. The index stood at 41.4 in December 1935 and 448.4 in December 1994, an increase of 1,083 percent. The Index itself has been devalued twice, first in 1967 and again in 1989, so that the December 1994 figure reported for the Consumer Price Index is only 149.7.

10. For 1935, the author. For 1954, Derek Bok, *The Cost of Talent* p. v (New York, The Free Press, 1993).

11. "The NLJ 250," *The National Law Journal* (Oct. 9, 1995).

12. D. Bok, *supra* note 10, at 224.

13. Altman Weil Pensa, *1994 Survey of Law Firm Economics* (Newtown Square, Pa.).

14. William James, "Spencer's Definition of Mind," *Writings 1878–1899*, 894, 900, 906 (New York, The Library of America, 1992).

15. James, *supra* note 14, "The Knowing of Things Together," p. 1057.

16. C. D'Este, *Patton: A Genius for War* 377–78, 415–16, 421–22, 540 (New York, HarperCollins, 1995). General Marshall had noted before World War II: "George will take a unit through hell and high water. But keep a tight rope around his neck" (pp. 377–78).

CHAPTER 4. THE DECLINE OF COST EFFECTIVENESS WITHIN THE LARGE LAW FIRM

1. *Bright and National Education Corp.*, American Arbitration Association, Los Angeles, 72–116–0802–89 (1990).

2. R. Gilson and R. Mnookin, "Coming of Age in a Corporate Law Firm," 41 *Stan. L. Rev.* 569, 589, 590 (1989).

CHAPTER 5. THE MAGIC OF THE EMPEROR'S NEW CLOTHES SUSPENDS THE LAW OF SUPPLY AND DEMAND

1. M. France, "Give Us an Estimate," *California Lawyer* 27 (March 1994).

2. California State Treasurer Matt Fong, on election to office, announced that while recognizing Orrick Herrington as chief bond counsel he would build a team of firms to compete for this work in the future. *Los Angeles Daily Journal* (April 24, 1995). Nevertheless, the firm's dominance of its field continues. *Los Angeles Daily Journal* (October 15, 1996).

3. *Goldfarb v. Virginia State Bar*, 421 U.S. 773 (1975).

4. *Supreme Court of New Hampshire v. Piper*, 470 U.S. 274 (1985).

5. R. Abel, *American Lawyers* 112–14 (New York, Oxford University Press, 1989).

6. Abel, *supra* note 5, at 247.

7. Committee on Ethics and Professional Responsibility, American Bar Association, Formal Opinion 93–379 (1993).

8. For California, see statutory organization of the State Bar, *California Business and Professions Code*, §§ 6010 ff.; creation of a full-time State Bar Court for lawyers' discipline, *California Business and Professions Code*, §§ 6079.1 ff.; investigation and discipline of judges by a Commission on Judicial Performance, California Constitution, Art. 6, Sec. 8; improvement in administration of justice by a Judicial Council, California Constitution, Art. 6, Sec. 6.

For transfer of responsibility for lawyer discipline in Illinois and Michigan, see M. Powell, "Professional Divestiture: The Cession of Responsibility for Lawyer Discipline," *ABA Research Journal* 31, 34 (Winter 1986).

CHAPTER 6. EXCESSIVE LEGAL FEES: THE COUNT DRACULA CLIENTS CANNOT STAKE

1. M. Jacobs, "Lawyers and Clients," *The Wall Street Journal* (Sept. 18, 1995).

2. Observations that follow are based on the author's experience as lawyer and judge. His conclusions are paralleled by those of the legal consulting firm of Altman Weil Pensa, which in a 1991 study for Federal Deposit Insurance Corporation reported:

Hourly rates bear little relation to the results or value obtained for the client, they reward inefficiency, and they encourage the prolonging of matters.

We earlier pointed out a number of inefficiencies that commonly appear in hourly fee bills: too many lawyers assigned to a project; too many lawyers attending conferences, depositions, court hearings or trials; too much turnover of personnel assigned to a project; excessive discovery; time devoted to issues prematurely or to marginal problems; failure to take advantage of work product produced at an earlier time . . . ; preparation of long formal opinions (or letters) when short, informal memoranda (or telephone calls) would meet the needs of the client; excessive intra-office consultation; and extreme pressure on law firm associates to generate billable hours. *None of these activities even marginally improves the quality of the work being performed.* (emphasis added.)

The foregoing quotation is found in R. Litan and S. Salop, "Reforming the Lawyer-Client Relationship Through Alternative Billing Methods," 77 *Judicature* 191, 192 (1994).

An analysis of practices is found in W. Ross, "The Ethics of Hourly Billing by Attorneys," 44 *Rutgers L.R. 1* (1991).

A comprehensive collection of case law on some of these items appears in J. Schratz, "Billing Guidelines and Fee Disputes: A Case Law Review," 18 *Trial Diplomacy Journal* 159–178 (1995).

3. *Imcera Group, Inc. v. American Home Insurance Co.*, California Superior Court, Los Angeles, No. BC011005 (1993).

4. John P. Quinn, *Law Firm Accounting*, § 8.04 (N.Y. Law Publishing Co., 1986, 1993).

5. M. Galanter and T. Palay, *Tournament of Lawyers*, 107, 108 (University of Chicago Press, 1991), argue that leverage produces exponential growth.

6. *The Arbutus Corporation vs. Danregn Vindcraft A/S, Home Insurance Company, etc.*, California Superior Court, Los Angeles, No. C727913 (1995).

7. A. Stevens, "Ten Ways (Some) Lawyers (Sometimes) Fudge Bills," *The Wall Street Journal* (Jan. 13, 1995).

8. S. Beck and M. Orey, "Skaddenomics," *The American Lawyer* (September 1991). Karen Dillon, "Dumb and Dumber, Firms Are Still Nickel-and-Diming Clients," *The American Lawyer* (October 1995).

9. "Skaddenomics," *supra* note 8, at 94.

10. *Matz v. Cohen*, Los Angeles Superior Court, C697280 (1993).

11. D. Ricker, "Greed, Ignorance and Overbilling," *ABA Journal* 62, 66 (August 1994).

12. *Fairfax Savings Bank v. Weinberg & Green*, Montgomery County Circuit Court, Md., 97269, reported in *The Washington Post* (Sept. 11, 1995), and *The National Law Journal* (Oct. 2, 1995).

CHAPTER 7. EXCESSIVE LEGAL FEES: EVEN THE COURTS CAN'T STAKE DRACULA

1. See *Stryker Corp. v. Intermedics Orthopedics Inc.*, 898 F. Supp. 116 (1995), where the court reduced legal fees from $5.1 million to $3.2 million for excessive and duplicative hours. See also *In re McDonnell Douglas Equip. Leasing Lit.*, 842 F.Supp. 733, 736 (1994), where the fee application for $4 million was reduced to $2.5 million; *Spicer v. Chicago Bd. Options Exchange*, 844 F.Supp. 1226, 1233 (1993), where the fee application for $4.7 million was reduced to $2.9 million; *Van Vranken v. Atlantic Richfield Co.*, 901 F. Supp. 294 (1995), where the fee application for $30.7 million was reduced to $19.2 million; *U.S. Football League v. National Football League*, 887 F.2d 408, 409–11 (1989), where fees sought were $7.7 million, and fees awarded $5.5 million.

2. *Stanton et al. v. Embrey, Administrator*, 93 U.S. 548 (1876).

3. *In re Osofsky*, 50 F.2d 925, 927 (1931).

4. *Johnson v. Georgia Highway Express, Inc.*, 488 F.2d 714, 719 (1974).

5. *Hensley v. Eckerhart*, 461 U.S. 424, 430 (1983).

6. *California Rules of Professional Conduct*, Rule 4–200 (1992).

7. *Pennsylvania v. Delaware Citizens Council*, 478 U.S. 546 (1986).

8. *City of Burlington v. Dague*, 505 U.S. 557, 112 S. Ct. 2638 (1992).

CHAPTER 8. LAWYERS AND THEIR DISCONTENTS

1. *Los Angeles Daily Journal* (April 25, 1995).

2. 1994 survey of lawyers conducted for the California State Bar by the Institute for Civil Justice at RAND. *California Bar Journal* (San Francisco, November 1994); and 36 *Law Office Economics & Management* 44 (1995).

3. See G. Kanner, "Welcome Home Rambo: High-Minded Ethics and Low-Down Tactics in the Courts," 25 *Loyola of L.A. Law Review* 81 (1991). T. Zlaket, "Encouraging Litigators to be Lawyers," 25 *Ariz. State L.J.* 1, 3, 4 (1993). B. McGuire, "Reflections of a Recovering Litigator: Adversarial Excess in Civil Proceedings," 164 F.R.D. 283 (1996). R. Nelson, "Uncivil Litigation," *Researching Law*, ABF (Fall 1996).

4. RAND survey, *supra* note 2. M. Dolan, "Miserable with the Legal Life," *Los Angeles Times* (June 27, 1995).

5. "Dreary Paper Chase Vexes Legal Rookies," *The Wall Street Journal* (October 21, 1996).

6. *Los Angeles Daily Journal* (May 20, 1996).

7. Milton, *Paradise Lost*, Book I, 83, 84, 85. Burke, *Reflections on the Revolution in France* 224 (New York, Collier Press, 1909).

8. *The Oxford Peerage Case*, 82 English Reports 51, 53 (H.L. 1625). *Dictionary of National Biography*, Vol. V, p. 81 (Oxford University Press, 1968).

9. C. McCurdy, "Prelude to Civil War," in *California S. Ct. Historical Society Yearbook* 1, 8 (Berkeley, University of California Press, 1994).

CHAPTER 9. THE PERVASIVE PUBLIC DISTRUST OF LAWYERS

1. Carl Sandburg, "The Lawyers Know Too Much," *in Collected Poems*, 189 (Harcourt Brace, 1950).

2. *U.S. News & World Report* (Jan. 30, 1995).

3. William Holdsworth, *A History of English Law* Vol. II, 344–348, 380, 499 (London, Methuen, 1909).

4. Holdsworth, *supra* Vol. II, at 348.

5. Holdsworth, *supra* Vol. III, at 394–401, 520; Vol. V, at 201 (rev. 2d edn., Boston, Little Brown, 1937).

6. Roundtable sponsored by American Bar Association and University of Georgia School of Law, *American Bar Ass'n Journal* 113 (August 1995). Panel on using the media, sponsored by Association of Business Trial Lawyers, Los Angeles, December 1995.

7. RAND survey of California lawyers for California State Bar. *California Bar Journal* (San Francisco, November 1994).

8. California Judges Association, "Legislative Update" (San Francisco, February 1995).

9. For ancient Rome see Tacitus, *The Annals* Book III, 25, 28; W. Durant, *Caesar and Christ* 262, 279, 289, 292 (New York, Simon and Schuster, 1944); Gibbon, *The Decline and Fall of the Roman Empire* Chapter IV, p. 237 (Milman edn., London, John Murray, 1854).

For the modern business view see J. Nocera, "Fatal Litigation," *Fortune* (Oct. 16 and 30, 1995). The cover of the magazine identifies the subject of the article as "Lawyers from Hell."

10. *American Bar Association Report*, 112 F.R.D. 243, 254 (1986).

11. "CCM," *The American Lawyer* 72–79 (Winter 1994).

12. A. Stevens, "Ten Ways (Some) Lawyers (Sometimes) Fudge Bills," *The Wall Street Journal* (Jan. 13, 1995).

13. K. Shepherd, "Getting a Fix on Fees," *ABA Journal* 49 (January 1996).

14. *West's California Laws, Business & Professions Code*, §§ 6147, 6148.

15. $8.3 million payment of judgment in *Hopkins v. Dow Corning Corp.*, aff'd, 33 F.3d 1116 (1994), cert. denied, 115 S.Ct. 734 (1995), held up by disputes among plaintiff's lawyers. See summary of *Dow Corning v. Bolton* in *The Recorder* (San Francisco, Feb. 9, 1995).

16. *Korn v. Robins Kaplan*, Los Angeles Superior Court, BC136470 (1995), *Los Angeles Times* (Oct. 22, 1995); *The National Law Journal* (Oct. 23, 1995).

17. Cravath Swaine: General Development Corporation bankruptcy (Miami, Fla.). Fee application of $323,000 reduced by the court to $34,000. S. Beck and M. Orey, "Skaddenomics," *The American Lawyer* 3, 93, 94 (September 1991).

Skadden Arps: South Florida Water Management District representation. $1.6 million reduced to $0.5 million. "Skaddenomics," pp. 3, 92–93.

Weil Gotshal: Leslie Fay bankruptcy (New York). Forfeiture of $1 million fees. *The Wall Street Journal* (Jan. 10. 1995). MCorp bankruptcy (Houston, Texas). Fee reduced by $4.4 million. *The American Lawyer* 18 (November 1995).

Latham & Watkins: Fireman's Fund Insurance Co. litigation, San Diego. Law firm suit for $664,000 additional legal fees abandoned, and $1.5 million paid back by law firm to Fireman's Fund. "Skaddenomics," pp. 3, 94. False claims by partner of $300,000 client expenditures, *Los Angeles Daily Journal* (Dec. 4, 1995; April 16, 1996), *The American Lawyer* 60 (Sept. 1996).

Sidley & Austin: Bradley Trusts litigation, Milwaukee. Fee claim of $999,000 against Old Republic Insurance Co. settled for $350,000. "Skaddenomics," pp. 3, 95.

Winston & Strawn: False claims against clients for $784,000 by managing partner. *The Wall Street Journal* (Dec. 20, 1994).

Mayer Brown: Disbarment proceedings of partner who overbilled clients for $500,000. D. Ricker, "Greed, Ignorance, and Overbilling," *American Bar Ass'n Journal* 64–65 (August 1994). *The Wall Street Journal* (Aug. 14, 1995).

18. Gibson Dunn: *The Wall Street Journal* (July 31, 1995); *Shaffer v. Superior Court (Simms)*, 33 Cal. App. 4th 993 (1995). Oakland bankruptcy court fee rejection of 639 hours of 889 hours claimed for fee billing. A. Stevens, "Ten Ways (Some) Lawyers (Sometimes) Fudge Bills," *The Wall Street Journal* (Jan. 13, 1995).

19. "The NLJ 250," *The National Law Journal* (Oct. 3, 1994).

20. Winston & Strawn: *The Wall Street Journal* (Dec. 20, 1994). Rose Law Firm: *Los Angeles Times* (June 29, 1995).

21. S. Linowitz, *The Betrayed Profession* 34 (New York, Scribner's, 1994).

22. Order of U.S. District Court, *Allen, etc. v. The City of Los Angeles, etc.*, CV 91–2497 JGD (Tx) (C.D. Cal. 1995).

23. Linowitz, *supra* note 21, at 31, 34, 82, 105, 208.

CHAPTER 11. FIRST CHALLENGE: CLIENT CONTROL OF FEES

1. Bristol-Myers Squibb Company, *Annual Report* 30 (1993).

2. "What Lawyers Earn," *The National Law Journal* (July 10, 1995).

3. M. France, "Give Us an Estimate," *California Lawyer* 27–28 (March 1994).

4. *The Lawyer's Almanac 1995* (Aspen Law & Business, Englewood Cliffs, N.J.) reports four corporate law departments (State Farm, Liberty Mutual, General Electric, and AT&T) have over 400 lawyers.

5. A comprehensive review of these practices may be found in a report of the California State Bar, Corporate Law Department Committee, *Business Law News* 5–16 (Winter 1995). See also D. Ricker, "The Vanishing Hourly Fee," *ABA Journal* 66, 69 (March 1994). Many large corporations, such as Merrill Lynch, Proctor and Gamble, Bank of America, Hewlett-Packard, Campbell Soup, and

Pacific Telesis have compiled specific rules that govern all legal engagements. S. Beck and M. Orey, "Skaddenomics," *The American Lawyer* 96 (September 1991).

6. Price Waterhouse Law Firm and Law Department Services Group, "1993 Law Department Spending Survey."

7. *Shaffer v. Superior Court* (Simms), 33 Cal. App. 4th 993 (1995). In determining reasonableness of fees sought by law firms for services of paralegals, some courts have considered amounts paid to their paralegals and amounts of markups in determining reasonableness. *Telesphere Intl. Securities Litigation,* 753 F.Supp. 716, 720 (1990); *Continental Ill. Securities Litigation,* 750 F.Supp. 868, 889–93 (1990).

8. "Navigating the 90s," *The American Lawyer,* Special Supplement 41–44, 49 (Feb. 1994).

9. Z. Baird, "A Client's Experience with Implementing Value Billing," 77 *Judicature* 198–204 (January-February 1994).

10. "CCM," *The American Lawyer* 25 (February 1995).

11. Advertisement in *The Wall Street Journal* (Nov. 20, 1995).

12. *West's California Business and Professions Code,* §§ 6200–6206. California State Bar "Rules of Procedure for Fee Arbitrations" and "Guidelines and Minimum Standards for Mandatory Fee Arbitration," both found in *West's California Rules of Court 1996,* compact edn., 1273–92. In November 1995, ten other states had comparable laws. M. Jacobs, "Lawyers and Clients," *The Wall Street Journal* (Nov. 20, 1995).

13. Price Waterhouse, Law Department Services Group, "1995 Law Department Spending Survey," in *The National Law Journal* (Oct. 16, 1995).

CHAPTER 12. SECOND CHALLENGE: INCREASED COURT CONTROL OVER LEGAL PROCEEDINGS AND LAWYER CONDUCT

1. See *West's Annotated California Code of Civil Procedure,* § 601, Historical Note (1976). 28 *United States Code, Judiciary,* § 1870.

2. M. Belli, "The Adequate Award," 39 *Cal. Law Rev.* 1, 27, 30 (1951); M. Belli, *Modern Trials* Vol. 4, pp. 21–37 (Indianapolis, Bobbs Merrill, 1959).

3. *West's Colorado Revised Statutes,* Annotated, §§ 33–44–103 to 107 (1990). *Utah Code,* Annotated, §§ 78–27–51 to 54 (1979).

4. After the state law enforcement fiasco in the 1963 Kennedy assassination, Congress in 1965 made assassination of a federal officer a federal crime and provided that federal court jurisdiction could supersede state court jurisdiction. Title 18. *United States Code, Crimes and Criminal Procedure,* §§ 1751 (1965).

5. After racketeering came to be seen as a national threat that state law could not handle, Congress under its authority to regulate commerce adopted a comprehensive law to outlaw organizations engaged in racketeering activity punishable under state or federal law, including offenses of murder, gambling, bribery, extortion, loan sharking, and narcotics dealing, and it gave jurisdiction over criminal enforcement and civil penalty suits to federal courts. Title 18, *United States Code, Crimes and Criminal Procedure,* §§ 1961–1965 (1970).

6. When terrorism and use of weapons of mass destruction became a threat, Congress made such activities federal crimes and gave exclusive jurisdiction to

federal courts. Title 18, *United States Code, Crimes and Criminal Procedure*, §§ 2331–2339A (1990–1994).

7. For California, see California Constitution, Art. 6, Sec. 21; California Rules of Court, §§ 244, 244.1, 532, 532.1; Local Rules, Los Angeles Superior Court, Rule 12.18.

8. R. Smith, "Saving Ourselves from Being Lawyered to Death," *The Washington Post* (Sept. 24, 1995).

9. G. Kanner, "Welcome Home Rambo: High-Minded Ethics and Low-Down Tactics in the Courts," 25 *Loyola of Los Angeles L.R.* 81, 94–96 (1991); T. Reavley, "Rambo Litigators: Pitting Aggressive Tactics Against Legal Ethics," 17 *Pepperdine Law Review* 637 (1990); B. McGuire, "Reflections of a Recovering Litigator: Adversarial Excess in Civil Proceedings," 164 F.R.D. 283 (1996).

10. An example is the California Civil Discovery Act, *California Code of Civil Procedure*, §§ 2016–2036, modeled on Federal Rules of Civil Procedure, Rules 26 to 37. The California law covers roughly the same ground as the federal rules but is four times as long.

11. J. Chanen, "States Considering Discovery Reform," *ABA Journal* 20 (April 1995); T. Zlaket, "Encouraging Litigators to be Lawyers," 25 *Ariz. St. L.J.* 1 (1993).

12. *California Constitution*, Art. 6, Sec. 18 (1994), Art. 6, Sec. 8 (1995).

13. For Judge Wyzanski, see Memorial Service, 1987, 677 F.Supp. lxxiii. For Judge Yankwich, see Memorial Service, 1976, 438 F.Supp., lxvii. For Judge Pollack, see his handling of the Boesky-Milken civil fraud litigation found in *Arden Way Associates v. Boesky*, 660 F.Supp. 1494 (1987), *In re Ivan F. Boesky Securities Litigation*, 669 F.Supp. 659 (1987); 825 F.Supp. 623 (1993), 36 F.3d 255 (1994).

14. Local Rules, Los Angeles Superior Court, Rule 2.4 (1995).

15. *Browning v. Peyton*, 123 F.R.D. 75, 77, 79 (1988).

16. Both lodestar and percentage of recovery have been held acceptable methods for determining fees in common legal actions. *In re Washington Public Power etc. Litigation*, 19 F.3d 1291, 1295 (1994); *Swedish Hospital Corp. v. Shalala*, 1 F.3d 1261 (1993); *Dubin v. E. F. Hutton Group, Inc.*, 878 F.Supp. 616, 621, 624 (1995); *Telesphere Int'l. Securities Litigation*, 753 F.Supp. 716, 717, 721 (1990); Third Circuit Report, "Court Awarded Attorney Fees," 108 F.R.D. 237 (1986).

17. *In re Olson*, 884 F.2d 1415, 1426–29 (1989).

18. *Ramos v. Lamm*, 713 F.2d 546, 553–55 (1983).

19. *Bowling v. Pfizer, Inc.*, 922 F.Supp. 1261 (1996) and 927 F. Supp. 1036 (1996); *General Motors Pick-up Truck Fuel Tank Litigation*, 55 F.3d 768, 822 (1995); *Swedish Hospital Corp. v. Shalala*, 1 F.3d 1261 (1993). In *Rosenbaum v. MacAllister*, 64 F.3d 1439, 1447 (10 Cir. 1995), the court in reversing a fee award said the conscience of the court was shocked by an award equal to $900 an hour for every lawyer, paralegal, and law clerk involved.

20. *Bowling v. Pfizer, Inc., supra* note 19; S. Terry, "Going to the Head of the Class Action Settlement," *The Washington Post* (April 8, 1996); H. Reske, "Two Wins for Class Action Objectors," *ABA Journal* 36 (June 1996).

21. *Fed. Rules Civ. Proc.*, Rule 11. *California Code of Civil Procedure*, Sections 128.5, 128.7.

22. *Los Angeles Times* (April 13, 1995).

23. For First Amendment right of free speech and press (Pentagon Papers) see *New York Times Co. v. United States*, 403 U.S. 713 (1971). For Sixth Amend-

ment right of fair trial see *Sheppard v. Maxwell*, 384 U.S. 333, 363 (1966). Both sides are entitled to a fair trial, which includes protection of both sides against prejudicial publicity.

24. The "substantial likelihood of material prejudice" standard was formulated in 1967 by the American Bar Association in *Model Rules of Professional Conduct*, 3.6, which by 1991 had been adopted by thirty-two states and approved by the Supreme Court in *Gentile v. State Bar of Nevada*, 501 U.S. 1030, 1043, 1067–68, 1070, 1075 (1991).

In 1971 the Department of Justice adopted similar rules governing relationships of its personnel with the media; 28 CFR 50.2.

25. *Gentile v. State Bar of Nevada, supra* note 24, at 1043.

26. *Gentile v. State Bar of Nevada, supra* at 1075.

27. California State Bar, *Rules of Professional Conduct*, Rule 5–120, was adopted in 1995 in response to legislative and court pressures. See *West's California Rules of Court 1996*, compact edn., p. 1154.

28. *In California v. Menendez*, Los Angeles Superior Court, BA068880 (1994 and 1996), the admitted shotgun killings of both parents by their two sons, the first trial, conducted with television and daily televised defense counsel press conferences, ended in a hung jury. The second trial, conducted without television and with a gag order imposed on counsel, resulted in murder convictions of both defendants. For gag orders in the federal courts, see *Levine v. U.S. District Court*, 764 F.2d 590 (1985); *R&T News Ass'n v. U.S. District Court*, 781 F.2d 1443 (1986). See also J. Moses, "Legal Spin Control: Ethics and Advocacy in the Court of Public Opinion." 95 *Columbia Law Review* 1811 (1995); Annual Judicial Conference of Second U.S. Judicial Circuit, "Public Relations on the Courthouse Steps," 141 F.R.D. 573, 586–643 (1991).

CHAPTER 13. THIRD CHALLENGE: THE BITE OF COMPETITION

1. S. Brill, "Lopping Off a Third," *The American Lawyer* 5 (June 1993).

2. More than seventy American law firms with art collections ranging from fifty to 1,400 works have listed themselves in the International Directory of Corporate Art Collectors. *Los Angeles Daily Journal* (Sept. 11, 1995).

3. Los Angeles Superior Court Reporters Association, "Effective Utilization of Court Reporter Technology" (1995). And see *California Rules of Court*, Rules 980.3–980.6.

4. J. Mokyr, *The Lever of Riches* 87 (New York, Oxford University Press, 1990).

5. A. Cohen, "Technology 101, The Road Warriors," *The American Lawyer* 121 (June 1996); "Suitware—High Noon for High Tech," *California Lawyer* 33 (June 1996).

6. *The Record*, NYC Bar Ass'n 478, 479 (May 1994).

7. Lawyers are not the only profession feeling the effects of these new competitive forces. Similar forces have been at work on physicians' earnings during the transition from individual medical care to collaborative health care. Thomas Priselac, director of Cedars-Sinai Medical Center in Los Angeles, whose gross receipts in 1993 were $500 million, identifies the Center's cost-cutting program and expansion of outpatient facilities as driven by industry-wide pressure to

provide high-quality service at the lowest possible cost. Reportedly, the transformation is meeting bitter resistance from many of the Center's 2,300 physicians, specialists, teachers, and researchers. D. Olmos, "A Dose of Reality Hits Cedars," *Los Angeles Times* (Aug. 14, 1994).

8. *Judicature*, 189 (January–February 1994).

9. S. Brill, "Lopping Off a Third," *The American Lawyer* 5, 81 (June 1993).

10. *Lindsey v. Dow Corning Corp.*, MDL No. 926, CV 94-P-11558S (N.D. Ala. 1994).

CHAPTER 14. FOURTH CHALLENGE: RESTLESSNESS IN THE WORKPLACE

1. Robert Griffith, *The Politics of Fear* 259 (University of Massachusetts Press, 1987).

2. G. Hettrick, "Doing Good," *ABA Journal*, 77 (December 1992).

3. Thucydides, *History of the Peloponnesian War*, Book I, secs. 18, 138.

4. The Cravath Swaine firm hired 233 lawyers between 1964 and 1974, of whom only twenty became partners. R. Gilson and R. Mnookin, "Coming of Age in a Corporate Law Firm," 41 *Stan. L. Rev.* 567, 583 (1989).

5. Movement of lawyers in Los Angeles from Haight Brown to Dickson Carlson and then to Brobeck Phleger produced lawsuits among lawyers and law firms on both moves. *The National Law Journal* (Nov. 27, 1995). *Haight Brown v. Superior Court of Los Angeles*, 234 Cal. App. 3d 963 (1991).

6. See references in K. Penasack, "Abandoning the Per Se Rule," 5 *Geo. J. of Legal Ethics* 889, 890–92 (1992).

CHAPTER 15. THE SHAPE OF LAW FIRMS TO COME: PROFESSIONAL MANAGEMENT

1. For Chauncey statements see *Yale Alumni Magazine* 31 (May 1995).

2. *The American Lawyer* 80 (November 1995).

3. In 1994 a jury returned a verdict for $6.9 million punitive damages plus attorneys' fees against Baker & McKenzie (Chicago) for ignoring sexual harassment in its Palo Alto office. The sum, amounting to 10 percent of the law firm's net worth, was reduced by the judge to $3.5 million plus attorneys' fees. *American Lawyer News Service* (Dec. 5, 1994); *The Washington Post* (Dec. 4, 1994). For a compilation of cases on office romance, see L. Michaels and T. Thornburg, "Employment Law," *The National Law Journal* (April 1, 1996).

CHAPTER 16. THE SHAPE OF LAW FIRMS TO COME: INTEGRITY AND QUALITY CONTROL

1. For the Jones Day $51 million settlement in Phoenix, see E. Couric, "The Tangled Web," *ABA Journal* 64 (April 1993). For the Jones Day $52 million settlement in Los Angeles, see *Los Angeles Daily Journal* (May 2, 1996); *California Law Business* (July 29, 1996); and *Charter House Realty v. Jones Day*, Los Angeles Superior Court, No. BC049898 (1996). For Kaye Scholer, Paul Weiss, and Rogers

& Wells, see "The Tangled Web," *supra*; and 107 *Har. L. Rev.* 1547, 1609, 1610 (1994). For the $45 million settlement by Paul Weiss in 1993, see A. Frankel, "What Paul Weiss Didn't Want You to Know," *The American Lawyer*, 70 (December 1993). For Blank Rome and Venable Baetjer, see "The Tangled Web," *supra*.

2. *The History of Herodotus*, Book I, secs. 136, 139 (University of Chicago Press, 1952).

3. "Lawyers and Clients," *The Wall Street Journal* (May 1, 1995).

4. Dickens, *The Pickwick Papers* 237, 364, 401 (New York, Dodd Mead, 1944).

5. *Lincoln Savings and Loan Assn. v. Wall*, 743 F.Supp. 901, 920 (D.C. 1990).

6. *S.E.C. v. National Student Marketing Corp.*, 457 F.Supp. 682 (D.C. 1978); *In re National Student Marketing Litigation*, 517 F.Supp. 1345 (D.C. 1981); S. Linowitz, *The Betrayed Profession* 231–34 (New York, Scribner's, 1994).

7. *F.D.I.C. v. O'Melveny & Myers*, 969 F.2d 744, 114 S.Ct. 2048, 61 F.3d 17 (1995).

8. The three-dozen remark was supposedly made by the head of Root Clark Buckner & Ballantine, now Dewey Ballantine (New York), on learning of the Paramount Publix bankruptcy. T. Arnold, *The Folklore of Capitalism* 256 (New Haven, Yale University Press, 1937).

9. S. Brill, "The New Leverage," *The American Lawyer* 5 (July–August 1993).

10. See remarks of John W. Larson of Brobeck Phleger and David Boies of Cravath Swaine in "Navigating the 90s," *The American Lawyer*, Special Supplement 11, 16 (February 1994). See also comments by Guy Rounsaville, general counsel of Wells Fargo Bank, in M. France, "Give Us an Estimate," *California Lawyer* 27–28 (March 1994).

11. S. Fortney, "Am I My Partner's Keeper? Peer Review in Law Firms," 66 *Univ. of Colo. L. Rev.* 329, 366–67 (1995).

CHAPTER 17. THE SHAPE OF LAW FIRMS TO COME: COMPETITIVENESS AND JOB SATISFACTION

1. J. P. Quinn of Price Waterhouse, *Law Firm Accounting* § 11.05(2). (New York, Law Journal Seminars-Press, 1993). Quinn's illustration of accounting by profit centers shows a litigation department with a profit margin of 50 percent, a corporate department with 34 percent, and an estate department with 20 percent. Similar segment cost accounting can be employed to show specific client profitability (or loss), specific location profitability (or loss), and specific lawyer profitability (or loss).

2. "Navigating the 90s," *The American Lawyer*, Special Supplement 11 (February 1994).

3. D. Boorstin, *The Americans: The National Experience* 113 ff. (New York, Random House, 1965).

4. S. Linowitz, *The Betrayed Profession* 29 (New York, Scribner's, 1994).

5. *Bates v. Arizona*, 433 U.S. 350 (1977).

6. Newspaper ad: "Have you lost money with STRATTON OAKMONT through high pressure phone sales? We represent people who have. No Recovery—No Fee." A law firm name and an 800-number are given, but no address. *Los Angeles Times* (Dec. 5, 1995).

7. For example, Bogalusa, Louisiana, a one-industry town, suffered a chemical spill and resultant gas cloud that did not critically injure anyone. Thereafter the town was invaded by a small army of lawyers seeking clients and advertising compensable symptoms. Its inhabitants found themselves debating which was worse—the toxic leak or the lawyer glut that threatened to put the town's principal employer out of business. J. Katz, "Town Ponders Worse Fate: Toxic Leak or Lawyer Glut?" *Los Angeles Times* (Nov. 19, 1995).

8. *Florida Bar v. Went For It Inc.*, 115 S. Ct. 2371 (1995).

9. Advertisement of Littler Mendelson (San Francisco) in *California Lawyer* (March 1994).

10. R. Battey, "Loosening the Glue: Lawyer Advertising, Solicitation and Commercialism in 1995," 9 *Geo J. of Legal Ethics* 287 (1995).

11. Firm advertisements in *The American Lawyer*, CCM (June 1995), and in *California Law Business* (Jan. 8, 1996).

12. H. Stimson, *On Active Service in Peace and War* xviii (New York, Harper, 1947).

13. *Martindale-Hubbell Law Directory* (1996).

CHAPTER 18. L'ENVOI—VISIONS IN THE CRYSTAL BALL

1. *West's California Corporations Code*, § 13406; *West's California Business and Professions Code*, § 6165.

2. Reported activities in San Francisco of Judgment Purchase Corp., "California Law Business," *Los Angeles Daily Journal* (April 3, 1995). For a survey of financing of lawsuits, see "Litigation for Sale," 144 *U. of Pa. L. Rev.* 1529 (1996).

3. *California Federal Bank v. United States*, Court of Federal Claims, No. 92–138C, where the bank seeks to recover losses suffered when the government assertedly reneged on its promise of tax breaks for institutions that would take over ailing thrifts. *California Lawyer* 24 (January 1996); *Fortune* 20 (Aug. 5, 1996); *Winstar Corp. v. U.S.*, 64 F.3d 1531 (1995), aff'd; *U.S. v. Winstar Corp.*, 116 S.Ct. 2432 (1996).

4. Legal Services Plan of America, which has its headquarters in Schaumberg, Illinois, solicits customers by mail and claims over 1 million members.

5. See activities of Legal Research Network Inc., a Los Angeles-based company specializing in outsourcing legal research. *The National Law Journal* (Nov. 13, 1995).

6. I. Wilson, *Shakespeare: The Evidence*, 192, 285–86, 365 (New York, St. Martin's Press, 1993).

7. William Holdsworth, *A History of English Law* Vol. IV, pp. 268–71 (2d edn., Boston, Little Brown, 1937); Vol. VI, pp. 478–93 (London, Methuen, 1924).

8. C. Klein, "Gold Rush, Thin Stakes," *The National Law Journal* (Aug. 12, 1996); "The Globalization of Corporate Law," *The Economist* (Nov. 23, 1996).

9. M. Glendon, *A Nation Under Lawyers* 12, 13, 29, 288 (New York, Farrar, Straus, 1994): "The spirit of Philadelphia has yielded to the spirit of Palm Beach." A. Kronman, *The Lost Lawyer* 2–4, 272, 283, 295, 353–54 (Cambridge, Mass., Harvard University Press, 1993): "The demise of an older set of values," p. 2.

10. R. Posner, "The Material Basis of Jurisprudence," 69 *Indiana Law Journal*

1, 28–36 (1993); *Overcoming Law* Chap. 1 (Cambridge, Mass., Harvard University Press, 1995). R. Abel, *American Lawyers* 118, 243 (New York, Oxford University Press, 1989), lauds the "erosion of professional control."

11. For composition of the California State Bar Board, *West's California Business & Professions Code*, §§ 6011, 6013.5. For composition of the California Commission on Judicial Performance, *West's California Constitution*, Art. 6, sec. 8 (1995).

12. S. Linowitz, *The Betrayed Profession* 163–66 (New York, Scribner's, 1994).

13. J. Fitzpatrick, "Legal Future Shock: The Role of Large Law Firms by the End of the Century," 64 *Indiana Law Journal* 461, 467 (1989).

14. M. Geyelin, "Smoking Guns," *The Wall Street Journal* (March 28, 1996).

15. S. Linowitz, *supra* note 12, at 29.

16. C. Albert, "The Lawyer-Director: An Oxymoron?" 9 *Geo. J. of Legal Ethics* 413 (1996).

17. In 1995 Morgan Lewis had a total of 786 lawyers, 211 in Philadelphia, 210 in Washington, 197 in New York, eighty-six in Los Angeles, and the remainder in seven other offices. "The NLJ 250," *The National Law Journal* (Oct. 9, 1995).

18. The Hongkong and Shanghai Banking Corporation survived the loss of its Shanghai market by developing a global banking system, and as a British corporation named HSBC Group it is well positioned to survive China's takeover of Hong Kong; *The Economist* (Sept. 7, 1996).

19. "The Mayo Clinic Story," Mayo Foundation For Medical Education and Research (1996).

20. S. Bundy, "Commentary on *Pennzoil v. Texaco*," 75 *Virginia L. Rev.* 335 (1989); *Pennzoil v. Texaco*, 729 S.W. 2d (Texas Ct. App. 1987); c.d. 108 S.Ct. 1305 (1988); dismissed per settlement, 748 S.W. 2d 631 (Texas Ct. App. 1988).

Index

About the Author

MACKLIN FLEMING is a retired Justice of the California Court of Appeal, currently sitting by assignment on the Los Angeles Superior Court. A graduate of Yale College and Yale Law School, he has divided his 55 years of legal experience between public and private practice in California, New York, and Washington, D.C., and trial and appellate judging on the California bench. He is the author of two previous books, *Of Crimes and Rights* (1978) and *The Price of Perfect Justice* (1974).